luscious **creamy** desserts

luscious creamy desserts

BY LORI LONGBOTHAM : Photographs by France Ruffenach

dedication

For Auntie Jean, always my favorite, with a lifetime of thanks.

acknowledgments

A great big thank you to Bill LeBlond, Amy Treadwell, and Judith Sutton. And to Jerry Goldman; Steve, Liz, and Sarah; Ellen McGill; and the Perrys. My gratitude for lots of fun and kindness also to Deborah Mintcheff, Barbara Ottenhoff, Barbara Howe, Jean Pellegrino, Marie Regusis, Joanna and Leigh, Sabra Turnbull, Cliff Burnstein, Lisa Troland, Rosie and Sprocket, Val Cipollone, Tracey Seaman, Jim Standard, Diana Sturgis, Sarah Mahoney, Honey Jeanne Laber, Kate Reese, Kathy Blake, Miriam Brickman, Amy Albert, Kim Masilbay, Rebecca Freedman, Jena Myers and her parents, Jon and Debby, Eugenia Escobar, and my cousin, the lovely Catherine Longbotham.

Text copyright © 2008 by Lori Longbotham.
Photographs copyright © 2008 by France Ruffenach.

Library of Congress Cataloging-in-Publication Data available.

ISBN 978-0-8118-5562-4

Manufactured in China.

Prop styling by Emma Star Jensen
Food styling by Elisabet der Nederlanden
Designed by Amber Reed and Kim Cullen

10 9 8 7 6 5 4 3 2 1

Chronicle Books LLC
680 Second Street
San Francisco, California 94107

www.chroniclebooks.com

CONTENTS

introduction

Who can resist luscious creamy desserts? They are the world's favorite comfort food. And that's saying a lot, since comfort foods are our most beloved of all. I think of creamy desserts as the teddy bears of the dessert world. A dessert may be flavored with chocolate, lemon, berries, or whatever —but our true favorites, the dishes that touch our hearts and stay there, the desserts we are always pleased to see sitting in front of us, are creamy.

Desserts are for pleasure. They are indulgences and luxuries, and we count on them to raise our spirits. And what could raise a mood or spirit better than a luscious creamy dessert like a quivering panna cotta, a rich butterscotch pudding, a caramel apple shortcake, or a Venetian-style fried custard? Many creamy desserts have a pristine simplicity—neither the techniques nor the ingredients are elaborate—and yet the potential for satisfaction, for pleasure, even for consolation, is huge. When we're served them, we feel safe and loved, and when we prepare them and serve them to others, we feel generous and nurturing.

This selection of desserts is not only a celebration of our favorite texture, it's also a celebration of flavors. While all the desserts are luscious and creamy, they are *not* all vanilla, or all white. Here are desserts with gorgeous, vibrant colors and bold flavors, along with others that are delicate and pale. It's no longer a vanilla world! Classic vanilla custard sauce is fantastic, but mango custard sauce is just as good as the original. It's even better with some desserts.

LUSCIOUS CREAMY DESSERTS includes desserts flavored with fruits and berries, including many types of citrus, dried fruits, and tropical fruits. You'll also find herbs, spices, and aromatics like tarragon, coriander seed, ginger, and licorice. Other flavorings include nuts of all kinds, liqueurs, and lots of chocolate, caramel, and coffee.

Just what defines a creamy dessert? To me it's any dessert that feels creamy in your mouth. It may not have heavy cream in it, but the creaminess is there. It may instead include mascarpone, half-and-half, crème fraîche, ricotta, yogurt, or sour cream. Or take lemon curd. It's definitely creamy, but the creaminess comes from egg yolks and butter, not cream. Lemon curd is essentially a custard that is made with butter instead of cream. Yet what is butter? Churned cream.

Some of the recipes in **LUSCIOUS CREAMY DESSERTS** are amazingly easy, while others are for more experienced cooks or for show-off occasions. There are both recipes for traditional desserts and fresh ideas for contemporary ones.

For me, creamy means caramel just as much as custard. Caramel is sweet and creamy, but dark caramel has an appealing bittersweet edge. It's the balance and complexity of flavors that makes it compelling. And a caramel sauce or syrup is a great foil for many creamy desserts. Think of the way the caramel that lines crème caramel offers the perfect bittersweet foil to the creaminess of the custard. Please take note also of the **Caramel-Coated Strawberries** (page 148)—their crisp, very thin coating of dark caramel really enhances the flavor of the berries as well as the look of the plate. They are a real treat.

Creamy desserts call out for contrast—crisp cookies on the side, crunchy praline on top, toasted candied nuts, an icy granita, a tart fruit sauce, or ripe fresh fruit and berries. You'll find lots of those contrasts here. I'm very fond of the **Lemon Crunch** (page 146), which is the quickest and easiest recipe in the book. Just crush a few of those rough-looking brown sugar cubes (like the ones served in upscale restaurants with coffee and tea) and stir in freshly grated lemon zest. The flavors come together in a wonderful way, and a sprinkle on top of a creamy dessert just before serving adds a very pleasing aromatic and fresh-tasting crunch.

Praline is a cousin to caramel. Shards of it, looking like shiny pieces of glass, make a grand garnish. Crisp, crackly coarsely or finely ground praline can be sprinkled over or into many creamy desserts. In fact, I had to keep myself from recommending praline for almost every one of these recipes. But please know you're encouraged to use praline with abandon.

You will find desserts here that are just the thing for a weekday when you, or someone you love, needs comfort. But when you want to celebrate, you have many choices—try the **Cannoli Cheesecake** (page 51), say, or the **Roasted Banana Ice Cream** with **Pecan Praline** (page 98), or the **Chocolate-Lemon Cream Cake with a Hat** (page 37). For more restrained occasions, try **Greek Yogurt with Sour Cherry Preserves, Walnuts, and Honey** (page 84), **Brown Butter–Crème Fraîche Pound Cake** (page 43), or **Espresso Granita con Panna** (page 109). Sometimes you just must have something luscious, creamy, and delectable, and you are sure to find the recipe here.

all about cream and other dairy products

Dairy products are produced from milk, mostly from cows but also from other animals such as goats and sheep. Not only delicious, they are high-energy-yielding foods, our richest source of calcium, and very nutritious. They are high in protein, B vitamins, selenium, zinc, phosphorus, potassium, and magnesium. And most dairy products are fortified with vitamin D.

Cream is a product of stillness. It is simply the part of milk that has a far greater concentration of fat than milk as a whole, and it rises through the body of the liquid to form that thick ivory layer at the top.

Most milk today is homogenized, using a process that forces the milk through a filter under very high pressure, which reduces its fat globules to around a quarter of their original size. These smaller particles are evenly dispersed throughout the liquid, where they are held in place by the milk's network of proteins.

Dairy products are categorized by the amount of fat they contain, as you will see from the following.

WHIPPING CREAM

Whipping cream contains 30 to 36 percent butterfat. To be whipped by whisking it with air, cream must contain at least 30 percent fat. When cream is whipped, air bubbles are trapped in a network of fat droplets, and it roughly doubles in volume. (The whipped cream produced by a canister with a nozzle propelled by nitrous oxide is four times the original volume of the cream.) Whipped cream is said to have been created in 1671 by chef François Vatel for a banquet for Louis XIV, but it probably existed long before then.

If you have a choice between pasteurized and ultrapasteurized cream, choose the former. Ultrapasteurized cream has a much longer shelf life than pasteurized, but because it has been heated to a higher temperature in processing, it tends to be less fresh-tasting. It also takes longer to whip, and the volume isn't as great.

HEAVY CREAM

Heavy cream (sometimes called manufacturing cream) contains at least 36 and up to 40 percent butterfat. It whips faster than whipping cream and is more stable when whipped. It is actually better for whipping, despite whipping cream's name, but because it can be overbeaten in a flash, turning to butter before your very eyes, and because the higher butterfat content makes it more expensive, it is not generally available at the retail level. It can be found through restaurant suppliers and some specialty foods shops. Most of the "heavy cream" in our supermarkets is actually whipping cream.

LIGHT CREAM

Light cream, also known as coffee or table cream, is not generally used for desserts. It has 18 to 30 percent fat.

HALF-AND-HALF

As its name indicates, this is simply half milk and half cream. It must contain at least 10½ percent butterfat, but no more than 18 percent. It cannot be whipped.

MILK

Milk is graded by the amount of fat that it contains. Use only whole milk in these recipes.

BUTTERMILK

Today low-fat milk is fermented with bacteria to make buttermilk. It is often the same type of bacteria used in making sour cream.

EVAPORATED MILK

Evaporated milk is fresh homogenized milk that has been heated until 60 percent of the water has been evaporated. The high heat used gives this canned product a cooked flavor with a bit of caramel, and it is slightly darker than fresh milk. Evaporated milk can be mixed with equal parts water as a substitute for fresh milk, but in the United States it is used mostly in making desserts. It's less concentrated than condensed milk and it almost never has sugar added. It requires more processing than condensed milk, since the sugar in condensed milk inhibits bacterial growth. It was developed by Gail Borden Jr. in 1852.

CONDENSED MILK

Also known as sweetened condensed milk, this canned product is milk that has had much of its water removed by evaporation and sugar added to extend shelf life. It includes only fresh full-fat milk and sugar. It's a thick, sweet product that can last for years without refrigeration. It was developed in 1865 by Gail Borden Jr., using a method the Shakers developed to condense fruit juice. Borden's Eagle Brand is still sold today.

SOUR CREAM

Sour cream, which is made from heavy cream, contains 15 to 20 percent fat. It gets its characteristic tang and thick texture from the lactic acid created by the bacteria used as a culture.

CRÈME FRAÎCHE

Crème fraîche, which translates as "fresh cream," is a thick and voluptuous French cultured cream, similar to sour cream but richer, with a minimum of 30 percent butterfat.

Crème fraîche is a specialty of Normandy. To my mind, it's one of the very few things that are better than heavy cream. Not as tangy as sour cream, or as thick, it is slightly fermented and has a subtle ripened, somewhat nutty flavor and a rich, velvety texture. It adds a depth of flavor and creaminess without being heavy or overwhelming. It has a longer shelf life than heavy cream and can even be frozen. It can be lightly whipped if chilled, and, unlike sour cream, it will not curdle when boiled. You'll find a recipe for crème fraîche on page 12.

MASCARPONE

The devastatingly rich Italian cream cheese, from the Lombardy region, is probably best known as one of the main ingredients in tiramisu. Fresh-tasting, rich, and creamy, it has a fat content of about 70 percent.

MEXICAN CREMA

Crema, available in Mexican and other Hispanic groceries, is similar to crème fraîche and is a good substitute.

BRITISH CREAMS

Many argue that the best cream in the world is found in the United Kingdom. British half cream has 12 percent butterfat, single cream (also known as pouring cream) has 18, and medium cream has 25. Heavy whipping cream has at least 35 percent

and England's gorgeous double cream is 48 percent butterfat.

Cream from Jersey cattle, typically found in Devon and Cornwall in the southwest of England, contains natural carotenoid pigments that come from the plants the cows eat, which gives the milk the color of pale buttercups. Jersey cream is often used to make clotted cream, which is made by heating unpasteurized milk and skimming off the yellow crust that forms. Beloved by many, the thick cream has a texture that is almost like butter, although it is too soft to slice, but unlike butter, it tastes of cream, not fat. Clotted cream has a warm golden color and a smooth, rich texture. Unlike crème fraîche, it is sweet, not at all tart. The fat content is very high, at a minimum 55 percent. It's classic with fresh fruit, with scones and preserves, and as a filling for pastries or sponge cake layers. I've tried to make clotted cream and have not had good results, but it is widely available at specialty foods stores.

RICOTTA CHEESE

Fresh ricotta has a clean, cool, bland taste and a texture that is substantially superior to the commercially made cheese. It is a great treat when whirled in a food processor until perfectly smooth and served with fruit. You'll find a recipe for making your own on page 13.

crème fraîche

MAKES ABOUT 1 CUP

An ancient food, yogurt is made by fermenting milk with bacteria. The fermentation of the milk sugar, lactose, produces lactic acid, which acts on the milk to give yogurt its thick texture and its tang. It can be made from any milk, but modern production mostly uses cow's milk; however, sheep's and goat's milk versions are available in specialty foods stores and many supermarkets.

Greek yogurt is made with some cream as well as milk, so it can have up to 18 percent butterfat, much higher than yogurts made with milk only or reduced-fat milk. It is sometimes made with sheep's milk. It has an ultracreamy, smooth texture and a very fine flavor. Give it a try in the Greek Yogurt with Sour Cherry Preserves, Walnuts, and Honey on page 84.

You can buy crème fraîche, but I find it expensive, and since it's not available in my neighborhood, I prefer to make it. My favorite way is to culture heavy cream with store-bought crème fraîche and keep it in my refrigerator almost ad infinitum, like a sourdough starter. The longer you leave it at room temperature to ferment, the tangier it will be. Sweeten it with a bit of confectioners' sugar if you'd like, gauging it against the sweetness of the dessert you'll be serving it with.

Sour cream with live cultures is widely available in health and specialty foods stores. This recipe can be doubled or tripled easily.

½	cup heavy (whipping) cream
½	cup crème fraîche or sour cream with live cultures

Pour the cream into a glass jar with a tight-fitting lid and spoon in the crème fraîche. Let sit on the counter, with the lid slightly ajar, until the mixture thickens, from 4 to 24 hours, depending on the weather. Refrigerate, tightly covered, until ready to use.

fresh ricotta cheese

MAKES 2 CUPS

At the Regaleali cooking school in Sicily, I had delectable made-that-morning ricotta cheese topped with the house grapefruit preserves. Wow. I've never thought of ricotta in quite the same way since. Theirs was made with sheep's milk, so it had a terrific flavor; make some with goat's milk from the supermarket sometime, and you'll see what I mean. This is what they use to fill real Italian cannoli.

You'll need a large strainer and cheesecloth.

8	cups (½ gallon) whole milk
1	cup heavy whipping cream
½	teaspoon salt
3	tablespoons fresh lemon juice

STEP 1 Line a large, coarse strainer with two layers of damp cheesecloth and set it over a large glass measure or bowl.

STEP 2 Bring the milk, cream, and salt just to a boil in a large saucepan over medium-high heat, whisking occasionally. Add the lemon juice, reduce the heat, and simmer, whisking constantly, for about 2 minutes, until the mixture curdles. Pour into the lined strainer and let drain at room temperature for 1 hour.

STEP 3 Discard the liquid whey and refrigerate the ricotta, tightly covered, for up to 2 days.

custard 101

If you have any trepidation about making custard, this quick tutorial will allay your fears. Many recipes for custard and its cousins make it sound as though the process is full of pitfalls and dangers. Well, that is not true. Making custard is actually easy, and although the method is not entirely foolproof (what is?), anyone can do it. It's one of the best cooking techniques to have in your skill bank, and once you understand the process and have made a custard or two, you will see how beautifully simple it is. It's all about temperature and not letting the eggs get too hot: gentle heat is the secret to cooking eggs.

The science is also very simple: gently heating the eggs thickens the milk or cream (or half-and-half). Stirred custards, such as rice pudding, custard sauce, and lemon curd, are on cooked on top of the stove. They are based on eggs or egg yolks and milk or cream, with a flavoring. Eggs and milk (or cream) are both very high in protein. When proteins are heated, their molecules unwind, with their bonds sticking out (can you picture that?), and when they run into other unwound proteins, they link together to form a gel. If the mixture gets too hot, however, the bonds tighten and squeeze out the liquid, resulting, in the case of custard, in scrambled eggs and liquid. All you need to do to keep that from happening is to heat the egg yolks gradually with a small amount of the hot liquid before adding it all. And then you whisk, and whisk, and whisk, while cooking the custard. Whisking or

stirring constantly keeps the temperature even, with no hot spots. If you suspect that the mixture is getting too hot—you may see little bubbles around the edges—just take the pan off the heat and continue whisking or stirring to cool it down. Using a good-quality heavy pan helps a great deal, heating the custard evenly and acting as insulation to keep it from getting too hot. Most of these recipes cook the custard over medium-low heat, but if a little lower is more comfortable for you, that's fine. (A little higher is probably not as good.) I use egg yolks instead of whole eggs in my custards because egg whites cook faster and at a lower temperature than yolks (picture an over-easy egg), and so there is less chance of overcooking the eggs when you don't use the whites. It also means you can make custards and curds without the need for a double boiler.

The classic test for doneness in a stirred custard is that it be thick enough to coat the back of a wooden spoon; when you run your finger across the custard on the spoon, it should leave a track. In these recipes I ask you to use a whisk for stirring the custard—so where does that leave you? Just have a wooden spoon close by for testing. But if you prepare enough custards, you will not need to use the spoon test; you will see the custard thickening on the sides of the saucepan and feel the custard thickening as you whisk. I'm a firm believer in constant whisking so no part of the custard sticks to the pan and overcooks or scorches. As soon as the custard is thick enough, pour it through a fine strainer set over a glass measure or a bowl. If you leave it in the hot pan, it will overcook; the custard will continue to thicken as it cools. Although it's not always necessary, I strain all of my custards. It takes just a second and ensures that your custard is perfectly smooth.

Although some custard recipes ask you to use a double boiler, it's not necessary, and it takes forever to make custard in one. Just keep your eye on the custard and follow the guidelines above.

Stirred custard will form a skin on top as it cools. That skin is actually casein, a milk protein, which has dried out from the heat. It's not enough to remove the skin, because another will form. Instead, to keep a skin from forming, whisk the custard occasionally until it is cool or place a piece of plastic wrap directly on the surface to keep out air.

Baked custards, like cup custard, cheesecake, flan, and crème caramel, have the same basic ingredients as stirred custards but are cooked in the oven. Instead of stirring, you use a water bath to protect the custard from direct heat. Baked custards that contain a starch, such as flour or cornstarch, don't need a water bath, because the starch will prevent the proteins from being overcooked.

The easiest way to cook in a water bath is to put the ramekins or baking dish in the roasting pan or large pan and fill the ramekins or dish with the custard mixture, then place the pan in the oven and carefully fill it with boiling water from a tea kettle to reach the height indicated in the recipe. The pan for the water bath should be large enough to allow an inch all the way around the ramekins or baking dish to prevent overcooking. Many recipes suggest placing a folded kitchen towel on the bottom of the pan to keep the bottoms of the ramekins or baking dish from getting too hot, but I find that unnecessary. I have never had a custard get too hot on the bottom unless it was cooked at too high a temperature or for too long.

To check for doneness, look at the baked custard. I look for edges that are set and a center that is still slightly jiggly. You can also use a table knife inserted into the center: if it comes out clean, the custard is done (once the egg proteins bind together, they are unlikely to stick to anything else). It can be easy to overcook custards at first, because you may think they are not cooked if they still jiggle, but they will actually continue to cook after they are removed from the oven. If you overcook them, they may scramble or "weep."

caramel 101

If you've never made caramel, it may seem intimidating, but, in fact, caramel isn't difficult. It's simply a matter of putting some sugar in a pan, maybe with water or corn syrup or another ingredient, and cooking it until it gets dark brown. Not burned, but dark brown, and fantastically bittersweet.

There are a few things that can go wrong, but they are easy to avoid. The sugar can crystallize as it cooks. To keep that from happening, you must be sure to dissolve it completely, every grain. Start by cooking the sugar and water over medium heat, stirring to help dissolve the sugar. Then bring the mixture to a boil and wash down the sides of the saucepan with a wet pastry brush if you see any crystals. Continue to wash down the sides of the saucepan to discourage crystallization as often as you think necessary, but keep in mind that the more water you add, the longer it will take the water to evaporate so the sugar can caramelize. Once you have brought the mixture to a boil, stop stirring—the agitation and aeration will result in cooling, which can cause crystallization. Adding just a tablespoon or two of light corn syrup or a teaspoon or two of lemon juice to the sugar mixture also helps prevent crystallization.

The only other things to watch for with caramel are not cooking it long enough or cooking it for too long. You want it to be a nice dark brown, not a pale beige; undercooked caramel will be too sweet and won't have that great caramel flavor. If it gets too dark, though, it can burn. Just take it slowly, keeping your eyes on the caramel and the sides of the pan, and test for color on a white plate when you think it's close to the color you want. The caramel will continue to darken even after you remove the pan from the heat.

Use a good heavy saucepan, so there won't be hot spots. Don't use a pan with a nonstick coating that won't do well at high temperatures. And make sure you use a saucepan that is large enough; the caramel will boil up as it cooks, and you need to allow extra room. Also, if your pan is too small, the sugar on the bottom

dulce de leche and cajeta

may caramelize before the sugar on the top dissolves. Add the sugar, then pour in the water, trying to dampen the sugar evenly. You can make caramel without adding water, but I find it best to add water because it helps the sugar dissolve more evenly. You have to wait for the water to evaporate before the sugar will caramelize, but there is less possibility of the sugar crystallizing and you don't have to watch it and stir constantly until all the sugar is dissolved. Add corn syrup or lemon juice, if you're using it. Then heat the mixture slowly over medium heat, stirring often, until all of the sugar is dissolved. Increase the heat to the highest heat possible, bring the mixture to a boil, and boil until the caramel starts to turn brown. It won't brown evenly, so you will need to swirl the pan a few times to blend it and even out the color. When it's just the shade you're looking for, remove the pan from the heat.

At this point, there are several directions you might take your caramel. You can add cream to make a caramel sauce (page 135), or add water to make a caramel syrup (page 138), or you could pour the hot caramel over toasted nuts to make praline (page 144).

Dulce de leche is the South American caramel. It's similar to Banoffee toffee in England, *confiture de lait* in France, *doce de leite* in Brazil, and *manjar blanco* in Chile. If it's made with part goat's milk, as it is in Mexico, it is called *cajeta*. It's a rich and decadent blend of milk and sugar that is cooked for a long time on top of the stove until it begins to caramelize and thicken. Chileans and Argentineans use it like butter or cream—as a cake filling, on toast, in profiteroles, and even in sandwiches. Mixed into whipped cream, it makes a perfect caramel cream frosting. Supposedly it is a Creole invention, but the recipe may have been brought to South America by the Spaniards or Portuguese. Whatever the story, it is the most beloved sweet in Latin America.

The ingredients are essentially the same everywhere it is made, but the proportion of milk and sugar may vary. Dulce de leche is available in some markets, but it's easy to make your own. If you use all cow's milk in this recipe, you will have dulce de leche; if you use some goat's milk, it will be cajeta. I prefer cajeta, because it has a more complex flavor. You may need to adjust the heat under the saucepan often, reducing it if the mixture starts to boil and increasing the heat if the mixture is not simmering.

STEP 1 Stir together ¼ cup of the whole milk, the cornstarch, and baking soda in a small bowl.

STEP 2 Combine the remaining 1 ¾ cups whole milk, the goat's milk (if making cajeta), and sugar in a large heavy saucepan and heat over medium-high heat, whisking, until the sugar is dissolved. (If making dulce de leche, substitute 2 additional cups whole milk for the goat's milk.) Whisk in the milk and cornstarch mixture and bring to a boil over high heat. Watch the mixture carefully—it may foam up. Reduce the heat and cook at a bare simmer, whisking frequently, for about 40 minutes, or until the mixture begins to thicken and there are some areas that begin to look like caramel. Then cook at a bare simmer, whisking occasionally, for another 40 minutes, until the mixture is a medium caramel color and slightly thickened; it will thicken further on cooling. Remove from the heat and cool in the pan for 15 minutes.

STEP 3 Pour the mixture through a fine strainer set over a medium glass measure or heatproof bowl. Cool completely and transfer to a glass jar. The caramel can be refrigerated for up to 3 months. Heat gently to thin before using, if necessary.

2	cups whole milk
1	teaspoon cornstarch
¼	teaspoon baking soda
2	cups goat's milk (for cajeta) or 2 cups additional whole milk (for dulce de leche)
1	cup sugar

baking basics

It's most important that you have fun, enjoy what you are doing, and not be anxious about the results. If your first efforts are not perfect to look at, you will find the encouragement to try again when everyone who tastes them raves about how delicious they are. You need not be a dedicated or experienced cook to produce delicious results.

All the recipes in this book are tried and tested, and changing the ingredients or methods will give different results. I suggest you follow the recipes carefully to begin with, and you will soon discover for yourself those that can easily be varied and how you might want to vary them.

Read the entire recipe before you begin. Then assemble the ingredients and equipment. Check to see if any ingredients need to be at room temperature before beginning.

Always use the best-quality ingredients.

Use the appropriate measuring cups for dry and liquid ingredients, and measure carefully. For liquids, use glass measuring cups with spouts. For dry ingredients, use metal cups that can be leveled off with a knife or spatula.

Preheat the oven for at least 15 minutes before baking. Be sure your oven temperature is correct; if it isn't, the baking time given in the recipes won't be reliable. Check the oven temperature often, using a mercury-type oven thermometer set on the middle oven rack. After preheating the oven, check the thermometer. If the temperature setting disagrees with the reading on the thermometer, adjust it up or down accordingly.

Baked goods should be baked in the middle of the oven unless otherwise indicated.

Most cakes, pies, and tarts should be cooled on wire racks (in or out of the pan, depending on the recipe) to prevent the bottom of the dessert from becoming soggy.

ingredients

BAKING POWDER AND BAKING SODA

Baking soda, pure bicarbonate of soda, is activated when it is mixed with an ingredient that is acidic, such as buttermilk. Baking powder, a combination of bicarbonate of soda, cream of tartar, and corn-starch, works no matter what liquid it's mixed with, as the cream of tartar provides the acidity. Don't let a batter made with baking powder or soda sit around before baking it, or you may not get optimal service from the leavener. Check the expiration dates on the packages before using, and be precise in your measuring, as too little or too much will not give the desired result.

BUTTER

Opt for the fullness of flavor and the creaminess of butter when making these desserts. Margarine doesn't taste good, it has an unpleasant mouth-feel, and it is loaded with trans fats (the most unhealthy fats of all). Always use unsalted, or sweet, butter for these recipes; salted butter is too salty for creamy desserts. (If you are observing Jewish dietary laws, you will want to substitute parve margarine for butter for nondairy meals. If you must use margarine instead of butter, use it in its least processed state; that is, don't use tub margarine, spreads, or butter substitutes, which contain more water than stick margarine and are not made for baking.)

EGGS

Use fresh Grade AA large eggs for these recipes; using a different size may mean disappointing results. Always purchase eggs from a refrigerated case and keep them refrigerated at home.

STICKY RICE

Sticky rice is the everyday rice of northeastern Thailand. An opaque short-grain rice, it is also called sweet rice or glutinous rice. You'll need it for the Thai-Style Sticky Rice with Coconut Milk and Mango (page 126).

SUGAR

The recipes in this book use many different sugars: confectioners' sugar, granulated sugar, light and dark brown sugar, and rough brown sugar cubes; a few recipes suggest dark muscovado sugar. Any brown sugar has the rich color and flavor of a bit of molasses, but dark muscovado sugar, from Mauritius, has the flavor of toffee. It can be used in recipes and is very nice sprinkled over unsweet-ened whipped cream or crème fraîche garnishing just about any dessert. You could also sprinkle creamy desserts with Demerara sugar, which has large crystals and is splendid when you want both a hint of sweetness and crunch.

PURE VANILLA EXTRACT AND PASTE

There is no quicker way to ruin a dessert than by using strong, artificially flavored extracts.

Vanilla—and other extracts—must be the real thing. In simple luscious creamy desserts, the vanilla you use is especially important. You want good, complex flavor and the aroma of fine vanilla, from the fruit of the vanilla orchid. If you prefer to use vanilla beans rather than extract, you might consider trying pure vanilla paste. It is a blend of pure concentrated extract and beans, including the seeds, in a natural sugar syrup, and it is easily measured. Give it a try, especially if you find the look of the tiny seeds in your desserts irresistible. Nielsen-Massey makes one with beans from Madagascar that is available at specialty foods stores and many supermarkets. None of the recipes in this book call for vanilla beans. The beans are incredibly expensive at the moment (and how much vanilla sugar can you make with the leftover pods?). I love the flavor and the flecks of little seeds, but my preference is for high-quality pure vanilla extract and vanilla paste.

It's best to add pure vanilla paste or extract to cool ingredients, because they both have an alcohol base and heat will release not only the fragrance, but the flavor as well.

equipment

BAKING PANS

Use shiny, not dark, baking pans. Baking sheets should fit into the oven with at least two inches of space between them and the oven walls so the heat can circulate freely.

CUSTARD CUPS AND RAMEKINS

Custard cups are individual Pyrex or ceramic oven-proof cups that are wider at the top than at the bottom. They are ideal for baked and molded custards and for serving stirred custards. Glass Pyrex cups are widely available in 6- and 8-ounce sizes, and the ceramic cups are available in many sizes.

Ramekins are small ceramic or glass ovenproof dishes that are shaped like tiny soufflé molds. They come in a wide assortment of sizes. This book uses 6-ounce ramekins exclusively—6 ounces of liquid will fill the ramekin to the very top. Ramekins often have a ridge on the inside, and I fill them just to that point.

ELECTRIC MIXERS

I used a handheld mixer for every recipe in this book that calls for a mixer. If you have a heavy-duty standing mixer, feel free to use it, but you don't need one for any of these recipes.

GLASS MEASURES

I use medium (4-cup) and large (8-cup) glass measures over and over when making creamy desserts.

Besides measuring milk, cream, or half-and-half with them, you can also strain a custard or similar mixture into one of these measures, making it very easy to pour the custard into ramekins, baking dishes, or an ice cream freezer. And, if you're not comfortable slowly pouring hot half-and-half or cream directly from the saucepan into a bowl of beaten eggs or yolks when making custard, either because the pan is heavy or because it doesn't have a spout, pour it into a glass measure and then into the eggs.

ICE CREAM MACHINES

There are now many reasonably priced machines available (at only about fifty dollars) that don't require the messy use of salt and ice, making the preparation of frozen desserts easy enough for a school night. Look for one that makes at least 1 quart.

MICROPLANE

The Microplane rasp grater's razor-sharp teeth shave lemon and other citrus zest instead of ripping and shredding, and it removes a lot more of the zest than other graters and gadgets. It also seems to never remove the white pith, which is a minor miracle in itself (that bitter white pith may be great for making marmalade set, because it contains a lot of pectin, but it can ruin a luscious creamy dessert). The Microplane is very comfortable to hold and use, with a well-balanced design, like a good knife. Once you use one, you'll never go back. They are widely available in kitchenware stores; for more information, go to their Web site, www.microplane.com. If you've ever left zest out of a recipe because you thought it was too much trouble, give the Microplane a go.

MIXING BOWLS

It's impossible to have too many mixing bowls. Stainless steel bowls are great for using as an improvised double boiler over a saucepan of hot water. Glass bowls are essential for use in the microwave, for melting chocolate or butter. For dessert making, you'll need at least one very large bowl for beating egg whites, cream, and the like. I find deep bowls far more versatile than shallower ones, especially when making creamy desserts.

PROBE OR CANDY THERMOMETER

A probe thermometer is very handy when making candy. You can leave the thermometer right in the saucepan, so you always know the exact temperature of the mixture, and it doesn't get in the way. You can even set an alarm to go off when your mixture reaches the temperature goal. If you don't have one, a candy thermometer will work just fine.

ROLLING PIN

The type you use is really a matter of personal taste—whatever you feel comfortable with. Your grandmother's pin, a wooden dowel type, or a

heavy ball-bearing pin with handles: any of these will be great.

RUBBER SPATULAS

One of the greatest recent advances in kitchen equipment is the development of heat-resistant rubber spatulas. Not having to worry about a meltdown is quite wonderful. Now you can use rubber spatulas for cooking, as well as for scraping down bowls while mixing, folding ingredients, and many other tasks. Very handy.

SIFTER

I don't use a sifter for sifting; I use a coarse strainer. Use whichever you like, but for the best crumb and accurate measuring, don't skip the sifting step when a recipe calls for it.

SILICONE BAKING MAT

For the Crunchy Nuts (page 145), I recommend using a silicone baking mat to keep the nuts from sticking to the baking sheet. The most common brand is Silpat from France, which can be found in kitchenware stores. You'll find many uses for yours once you have it in your kitchen.

STRAINERS

I use strainers often, to strain out tiny bits of overcooked egg and whatever else might get in the way of the perfect smoothness of a finished luscious creamy dessert. Have a few on hand, large and small, coarse and fine. A small fine strainer is also perfect for sifting confectioners' sugar or cocoa powder over a dessert just before serving.

WHISKS

These are very handy kitchen tools. Find one or two that feel well balanced and comfortable in your hand. I often use a whisk to aerate and mix dry ingredients; it's quicker and easier than sifting when sifting is not really necessary. I also use whisks for folding one component of a dish into another. Have both large and small whisks on hand. I find smaller, more flexible whisks are best for custards.

WIRE RACKS

A couple of large, sturdy wire racks are essential for cooling baked goods.

tips, techniques, and tricks of the trade

BEATING EGG WHITES

Always use an impeccably clean bowl and beaters. If I'm not absolutely confident that no vestige of egg yolk or other fat is lurking, I give the beaters and bowl a quick wash with a bit of vinegar and water. I've found it works best to beat at medium speed until the whites are foamy, then increase the speed to medium-high and beat to soft or stiff peaks as the recipe requires. For soft peaks, beat the whites just until, when the mixer is turned off and the beaters are lifted, the foam makes a peak that falls over immediately. For stiff peaks, beat until that peak stands straight up and stays there.

COOKING TIMES

When a range of cooking or baking times is given (for example, "Bake for 30 to 40 minutes"), always check for doneness after the first increment of time has elapsed and then continue to watch closely until done.

CREAMING BUTTER AND SUGAR

Use an electric mixer for creaming butter and sugar, and beat until the sugar is barely grainy and the mixture is light and fluffy. This can take a few minutes, so make sure to beat long enough. Begin with room-temperature butter.

CUTTING OUT BISCUITS

Pat out the dough to the desired thickness. Dip the biscuit cutter into flour and cut out the biscuits using a straight in-and-out motion, dipping the cutter into the flour again before cutting out each biscuit. Then gather together and pat out the scraps if necessary to cut out more biscuits.

FOLDING

Folding is used to combine certain ingredients, such as whipped egg whites, with another ingredient or mixture without deflating them. Use either a whisk or a rubber spatula. First add a small amount of the mixture you're folding in to the bowl and cut straight down through the center of the mixture to incorporate it, then turn the whisk or spatula toward you and lift up. Turn the bowl an inch or two and repeat, working around the bowl just until no streaks remain. Then add the remainder and fold in.

MEASURING BROWN SUGAR

Firmly pack the sugar into a metal measuring cup, pressing down on it firmly enough so that it will hold its shape when turned out. Use a small metal spatula or a table knife to level off the top.

MEASURING FLOUR

The way you measure flour for a dessert recipe is crucial to the final outcome. For these recipes, first stir the flour in the canister to aerate it, then spoon it into the measuring cup so that it mounds above the top and level the top with a metal spatula or table knife. (Always use a metal measuring cup for dry ingredients.) Dipping the measuring cup into the flour and scooping it out will give you a different amount of flour, and your results may be disappointing. Another flour caveat: 1 cup flour, sifted, is different enough from 1 cup sifted flour to affect the dessert. Pay close attention to whether the flour should be sifted before measuring or after, or both.

ROLLING OUT PIE OR TART PASTRY

Place the disk of dough on a lightly floured smooth work surface and sprinkle the dough and the rolling pin with flour. Roll out the dough with short, even strokes, working from the center out, lifting and turning the pastry as you roll. To transfer the pastry to the pie or tart pan, carefully fold it over the rolling pin, lift it up, and drape it over the pan, then ease it gently into the pan without stretching it. For sticky or hard-to-handle doughs, flour a piece of wax paper and put the disk of dough on it, flour the dough, and place another sheet of wax paper over the dough before rolling it out. Using wax paper is also good if crusts make you nervous and you need to build your confidence.

STRAINING

To strain a custard, purée, or other mixture, I find it's best to use two heatproof rubber spatulas—one inside the strainer, for pushing ingredients through, and a second one for scraping the bottom of the strainer to get everything that's been strained.

cakes

We gather around a cake with excitement, anticipation, and a feeling of togetherness. Even if it's not a special occasion, putting a cake on the table makes it seem like one. There are cakes in this chapter that will heighten all those feelings, cakes that are not only showstoppers but also celebrations in themselves. The Chocolate Coffee Dacquoise (page 40), a crisp, nutty meringue cake filled with creamy chocolate ganache and lots of ultracreamy coffee buttercream, makes any time a grand event. The impressive Chocolate–Lemon Cream Cake with a Hat (page 38) is whimsical and fun as well as unique—you've probably never seen a cake like it. It's a simple rich dark chocolate cake made with ground hazelnuts, topped with luscious lemon curd folded together with whipped cream and then a tall meringue "hat." The two layer cakes will charm anyone. The Passion Fruit and Cream Cake (page 32) is filled with a luxurious passion fruit curd and whipped cream. It's simple but very festive and beautiful. The Gorgeous Caramel and Cream Layer Cake (page 30) is fantastic: four layers of cake separated by voluptuous cream and caramel sauce, with a spiral design of caramel sauce on top. Every time I make it, I wish I could eat the whole thing. If you love chocolate, the Chocolate Truffle Cake with Cardamom Praline (page 35) is very dramatic and tastes as good as anything else on earth. The Brown Butter–Crème Fraîche Pound Cake (page 43) is rich and very simple, with an excellent crumb. The Creamy Rice Pudding Cake (page 45) is a baked rice pudding surrounded by a deep, dark caramel, homey and elegant at once.

gorgeous **caramel** and **cream** layer cake

SERVES 8 TO 10

This cake uses two of my very favorite things—soft, billowy cream and dark, rich caramel. It's easy to make this one look good. You could use Dulce de Leche or Cajeta (page 18) or Butterscotch Sauce (page 139) instead of the caramel, but I prefer the caramel sauce because of its deep, bittersweet flavor.

STEP 1 Position a rack in the middle of the oven and preheat the oven to 350°F. Butter two 8-by-1 ½-inch round cake pans and line the bottoms with parchment or wax paper.

STEP 2 Sift the flour 3 times onto a sheet of wax paper.

STEP 3 With an electric mixer on medium-high speed, beat the eggs, granulated sugar, and brown sugar in a large bowl for 8 to 10 minutes, until the mixture is very thick and pale and the volume has increased at least 3 times. Sift half of the flour over the mixture and fold in with a whisk just to combine. Repeat with the remaining flour. Drizzle the butter over the mixture, whisking just to combine. Divide the batter evenly between the 2 pans.

STEP 4 Bake for 20 to 25 minutes, or until the cakes begin to pull away from the sides of the pans. Cool for 10 minutes in the pans on a wire rack, then turn out of the pans and remove the paper. Turn right side up to cool to room temperature.

STEP 5 With an electric mixer on medium-high speed, beat the cream in a medium bowl just until it forms stiff peaks when the beaters are lifted.

CAKE

1 ¼	cups all-purpose flour
6	large eggs, at room temperature
¼	cup granulated sugar
3	tablespoons packed light brown sugar
½	cup (1 stick) unsalted butter, melted
1	cup heavy (whipping) cream
1	cup chilled Caramel Sauce (page 135)

STEP 6 Cut each cake horizontally into two layers with a long serrated knife. Transfer one layer to a serving platter. Spread ½ cup of the cream over it with a long metal spatula, drizzle with ¼ cup of the caramel sauce, and top with another cake layer. Repeat with 2 more layers. Place the top layer on top and spread with the remaining cream. Drizzle the caramel sauce over the top in a spiral pattern, letting some of it drip down the sides, if you like. Serve cut into wedges.

passion fruit and cream cake

SERVES 8 TO 10

Frozen passion fruit purée is available in Hispanic markets and many supermarkets. It's difficult to find fresh passion fruit, and the frozen purée is excellent, intensely flavorful, and inexpensive. Once you bring some home, you'll find many uses for it. Try putting a little in your iced tea or lemonade, or swirl it into your yogurt.

You could use the lime curd from the Lime Tart with Brown Butter Crust (page 55), instead of the passion fruit curd, for this cake—or use the passion fruit curd in the tart. You could also use the passion fruit curd to turn the Chocolate–Lemon Cream Cake with a Hat (page 37) into a Chocolate–Passion Fruit Cake. You'll have about a half cup of the curd left over from this recipe, and I'll bet smearing it on your morning toast will make you happy.

LUSCIOUS CREAMY DESSERTS

PASSION FRUIT CURD

½	cup (1 stick) unsalted butter
5	large egg yolks
½	cup sugar
½	cup thawed frozen passion fruit purée
	Pinch of salt
2	teaspoons fresh lime juice

STEP 1 To make the curd: Melt the butter in a medium heavy saucepan over medium-low heat. Remove the pan from the heat and whisk in the egg yolks, sugar, passion fruit purée, and salt. Return to medium heat and cook, whisking frequently at first and constantly toward the end, for about 10 minutes, until thickened.

STEP 2 Immediately pour the curd through a fine strainer set over a medium glass measure or bowl. Whisk in the lime juice. Let cool to room temperature, whisking occasionally; the curd will continue to thicken as it cools. Refrigerate, tightly covered, for about 2 hours, until thoroughly chilled and set. (The curd can be refrigerated for up to 1 month.)

STEP 3 Position a rack in the middle of the oven and preheat the oven to 350°F. Butter two 8-by-1 ½-inch round cake pans and line the bottoms with parchment or wax paper.

STEP 4 To make the cake: Sift the flour 3 times onto a sheet of wax paper.

STEP 5 With an electric mixer on medium-high speed, beat the eggs and sugar in a large bowl for 8 to 10 minutes, until the mixture is very thick and pale and the volume has increased at least 3 times. Sift half of the flour over the egg mixture and fold in with a whisk just until combined. Repeat with the remaining flour. Drizzle the butter over the mixture and whisk just to combine. Divide the batter evenly between the 2 pans.

STEP 6 Bake for 20 to 25 minutes, or until the cakes begin to pull away from the sides of the pans. Cool for 10 minutes on a wire rack in the pans, then turn out of the pans and remove the paper. Turn right side up and let cool to room temperature.

STEP 7 With an electric mixer on medium-high speed, beat the cream in a medium bowl just until it forms stiff peaks when the beaters are lifted. Transfer one cake layer to a serving platter. Spread ¾ cup of the passion fruit curd (reserve the remaining curd for another use) over the layer with a long metal spatula. Top with the cream, add the remaining cake layer, and dust the top generously with confectioners' sugar. Serve cut into wedges.

CAKE

1 ¼	cups all-purpose flour
6	large eggs
¾	cup sugar
¼	cup (½ stick) unsalted butter, melted
½	cup heavy (whipping) cream
	Confectioners' sugar for dusting

chocolate truffle cake with cardamom praline

SERVES 10 TO 12

This is a good example of how to add flavoring to a praline. If cardamom is not your favorite, try fennel or anise seeds—they're both terrific with chocolate.

1	cup blanched whole almonds
4	green cardamom pods
1	cup sugar
½	cup water
1	pound plus 10 ounces bittersweet or semisweet chocolate, chopped
2 ½	cups heavy (whipping) cream
3	large egg yolks

STEP 1 Preheat the oven to 350°F.

STEP 2 Spread the almonds on a baking sheet and toast for about 15 minutes, until golden brown and fragrant. Cool on the pan, then push the almonds close together, in a single layer.

STEP 3 Crush the cardamom and discard the pods. Heat ¾ cup of the sugar, ¼ cup of the water, and the cardamom seeds in a medium heavy saucepan over medium heat, stirring, until the sugar is dissolved. Increase the heat to high and bring the mixture to a boil, washing down the sides of the pan with a wet pastry brush if you see any sugar crystals. Boil, without stirring, and swirling the pan toward the end to even out the color, until the caramel is a dark amber color. Immediately pour the caramel in a circular motion over the almonds to coat them evenly. Let set for 15 minutes, or until cooled and hardened.

STEP 4 Break the praline into small pieces with your hands, and process until coarsely ground in a food processor.

STEP 5 Line the bottom of a 9-inch springform pan with wax paper.

STEP 6 Melt 1 pound 5 ounces of the chocolate with ½ cup of the cream and the remaining ¼ cup water in a heatproof bowl set over a saucepan of about 1 ½ inches of barely simmering water, stirring occasionally. Remove the bowl from the heat and whisk until smooth.

STEP 7 With an electric mixer on medium-high speed, beat the egg yolks and the remaining ¼ cup sugar in a large bowl for 8 to 10 minutes, until the mixture is very thick and pale and the volume has increased at least 3 times. Add the melted chocolate mixture in 3 batches, beating on medium speed just until combined. Set aside ⅓ cup of the praline for garnish. With a whisk or a rubber spatula, fold the remaining praline into the chocolate mixture. *continued ...*

chocolate truffle cake with cardamom praline ... *continued*

STEP 8 With the electric mixer on medium-high speed, beat 1 ½ cups of the cream until it begins to thicken. With a whisk, fold the cream into the chocolate mixture in 3 batches. Pour into the springform pan and smooth the top with a rubber spatula. Refrigerate, tightly covered, for at least 8 hours, or for up to 24 hours.

STEP 9 Place the remaining 5 ounces chocolate in a medium heatproof bowl. Bring the remaining ½ cup cream just to a boil in a small saucepan over medium heat, and pour over the chocolate. Let stand for 2 minutes, then whisk until smooth. Let cool to room temperature.

STEP 10 Remove the cake from the pan, peel off the wax paper, and transfer the cake to a serving platter. With a long metal spatula, cover the top and sides of the cake as smoothly as possible with the chocolate mixture. (If your kitchen is hot and the chocolate is too soft, refrigerate it for a few minutes, until it reaches spreading consistency.) Refrigerate the cake for at least 30 minutes, until the chocolate is set, or for up to 12 hours.

STEP 11 Sprinkle the top of the cake with the reserved praline, and serve cut into wedges.

chocolate-lemon
cream cake with a hat

SERVES 8 TO 10

This cake is adapted from a recipe by Joan Campbell, one of my favorite food writers and the grande dame of cookery in Australia. She calls it Winter Gâteau, but I couldn't bear to, because it is also lovely in summer. It's glamorous and fun, and because it's got such a great look, you should always let your guests see the cake before cutting it. Make sure to save the egg whites left from the curd for the meringue.

CAKE

1⅓	cups hazelnuts
¾	cup sugar
6	ounces bittersweet or semisweet chocolate, chopped
¾	cup (1½ sticks) unsalted butter, at room temperature
6	large eggs, separated
	Pinch of salt
	Pinch of cream of tartar
½	cup heavy (whipping) cream

STEP 1 Position a rack in the middle of the oven and preheat the oven to 375°F. Butter a 9-inch springform pan, line the bottom of the pan with parchment paper, and butter the parchment.

STEP 2 To make the cake: Process the hazelnuts with ½ cup of the sugar in a food processor until finely ground.

STEP 3 Melt the chocolate in a heatproof bowl set over a saucepan of about 1½ inches of barely simmering water. Remove the bowl from the heat and whisk until smooth. Let cool.

STEP 4 With an electric mixer on medium-high speed, beat the butter with the remaining ¼ cup sugar in a large bowl until light and fluffy. Reduce the speed to medium and beat in the egg yolks one at a time, beating well after each addition. Beat in the melted chocolate. Reduce the speed to low and slowly beat in the hazelnut mixture.

STEP 5 With clean beaters, beat the egg whites with the salt and cream of tartar in a large clean bowl just until they form stiff peaks when the beaters are lifted. Whisk about 1 cup of the egg whites into the chocolate mixture, then whisk in the remaining egg whites in 2 batches. Spoon the batter into the pan and smooth the top with a rubber spatula. *continued ...*

LEMON CURD

½	cup (1 stick) unsalted butter
6	large egg yolks
¾	cup sugar
3	tablespoons finely grated lemon zest
½	cup fresh lemon juice
	Pinch of salt

chocolate-lemon cream cake with a hat ... *continued*

STEP 6 Bake for 20 minutes. Reduce the heat to 350°F and bake for 20 to 25 minutes longer, or until a wooden pick inserted in the center comes out almost clean. Cool completely on a wire rack. The cake will fall slightly as it cools.

STEP 7 Meanwhile, make the lemon curd: Melt the butter in a medium saucepan over medium-low heat. Remove the pan from the heat and whisk in the egg yolks, sugar, zest, lemon juice, and salt. Return to medium heat and cook, whisking frequently at first and constantly toward the end, for about 10 minutes, until thickened.

STEP 8 Immediately pour the curd through a fine strainer set over a medium glass measure or bowl. Let cool to room temperature, whisking occasionally; the curd will continue to thicken as it cools. Refrigerate, tightly covered, for about 2 hours, until thoroughly chilled and set. (The curd can be refrigerated for up to 1 month.)

MERINGUE

6	large egg whites
	Pinch of salt
1	cup sugar
1	teaspoon distilled white vinegar
½	teaspoon pure vanilla extract

STEP 9 To make the meringue: Preheat the oven to 250°F. Line the bottom and sides of a 9-by-2-inch round cake pan with aluminum foil, letting it extend about 2 inches over the edges of the pan. Lightly butter the foil. Place the cake pan on a baking sheet.

STEP 10 With an electric mixer on medium-high speed, beat the egg whites with the salt in a large bowl just until they form soft peaks when the beaters are lifted. Add ¾ cup of the sugar about 1 tablespoon at a time, beating well after each addition, then beat just until the egg whites form stiff peaks. Beat in the remaining ¼ cup sugar, the vinegar, and vanilla.

STEP 11 Spoon the meringue into the cake pan and smooth the top with a rubber spatula. Bake for 1 ½ hours, or until pale golden brown. Using the foil, carefully lift the meringue from the pan and transfer to a wire rack to cool completely.

STEP 12 Just before serving, place the chocolate cake on a serving platter. With an electric mixer on medium-high speed, beat the cream just until it forms stiff peaks when the beaters are lifted. Fold in 1 cup of the lemon curd (reserve the remaining curd for another use). Spread the cream over the top of the cake with a long metal spatula, stopping about ¾ inch from the edges. Carefully lift up the meringue, remove the foil, and place the meringue on top of the cake. Serve cut into wedges.

chocolate coffee dacquoise

SERVES 8 TO 10

Whoever invented the dacquoise was a genius. The flavors are superb, the textures sublime. It's from the southwestern French town of Dax (whose residents are called Dacquois). For this version, the crunchy, nutty meringues are layered with creamy chocolate ganache and covered with smooth, creamy coffee buttercream. It makes a great birthday cake. Or a cake to celebrate the New Year. You could use hazelnuts instead of almonds, or a combination of nuts. For a gorgeous look, you might toss the sliced almonds with coarsely ground almond Praline (page 144) to coat the cake.

I use a probe thermometer for the buttercream; I keep it right in the saucepan, so I don't have to worry.

STEP 1 Position the racks in the top and bottom thirds of the oven and preheat the oven to 350°F. Trace three 8-inch circles on 2 large sheets of parchment paper (2 circles on one sheet, 1 on the other), and place the paper on 2 large baking sheets, tracing side down.

STEP 2 To make the meringues: Toast the blanched almonds on a large baking sheet for about 15 minutes, until golden brown and fragrant. Transfer to a plate to cool. Reduce the oven temperature to 250°F.

STEP 3 Pulse the toasted nuts in a food processor just until finely ground.

MERINGUES

2	cups blanched almonds, chopped
1 ½	cups sugar
2	tablespoons cornstarch
8	large egg whites, at room temperature
	Pinch of salt
1 ½	teaspoons pure vanilla extract
2	cups sliced unblanched almonds

STEP 4 Whisk together ½ cup of the sugar and the cornstarch in a small bowl, and set aside. With an electric mixer on medium speed, beat the egg whites in a large deep bowl until foamy. Increase the speed to medium-high, add the salt, and beat just until the egg whites form soft peaks when the beaters are lifted. Add the remaining 1 cup sugar 1 tablespoon at a time, beating well after each addition, and continue to beat just until the whites form stiff peaks. With a whisk or a rubber spatula, fold in the reserved sugar mixture in 3 batches. Fold in the vanilla. Fold in the ground almonds in 3 batches.

STEP 5 Spoon the meringue onto the paper circles (using about 2 ⅔ cups for each circle) and smooth with a spatula; you want them to be straight across the top, not domed in the center. Bake the meringues for 3 hours, or until medium golden brown, switching the baking sheets halfway through. Transfer the meringues, still on the parchment paper, to wire racks and cool completely. Increase the oven temperature to 350°F. *continued ...*

chocolate coffee dacquoise ... *continued*

GANACHE

1	cup heavy (whipping) cream or crème fraîche, homemade (page 12) or store-bought
8	ounces bittersweet or semisweet chocolate, finely chopped

STEP 6 Toast the sliced almonds on a large baking sheet for about 10 minutes, or until golden brown and fragrant. Transfer to a plate to cool.

STEP 7 To make the ganache: Bring the cream just to a boil in a medium saucepan over medium heat. Remove the saucepan from the heat, add the chocolate, and let stand for 2 minutes. Whisk until smooth, then transfer to a bowl and let cool to room temperature. Then refrigerate, tightly covered, until thick enough to spread, about 30 minutes.

STEP 8 Meanwhile, make the buttercream: With an electric mixer on high speed, beat the egg yolks with ½ cup of the sugar in a medium deep bowl for about 5 minutes, until very thick and pale.

STEP 9 Bring the cream, the remaining ½ cup sugar, and the espresso powder to a boil in a large saucepan over medium-high heat, whisking until the sugar and espresso powder are dissolved. Beating on medium-high speed, slowly pour half of the hot cream mixture into the yolks. Return the yolk mixture to the saucepan with the cream and whisk in the salt. Cook over medium heat, whisking constantly, for 6 minutes, or until the custard registers 170°F on a thermometer. Do not boil.

STEP 10 Immediately transfer the mixture to a large deep bowl and, with an electric mixer on high speed, beat for about 6 minutes, until cooled to room temperature. Beating on high speed, add the butter 1 tablespoon at a time, beating well after each addition. Transfer to a bowl and refrigerate, tightly covered, for about 45 minutes, until firm enough to spread. (If the buttercream gets

too cold after chilling, beat on high speed until smooth and spreadable.)

STEP 11 Peel off the parchment paper from the meringues. Reserve the best-looking meringue for the top layer. Place the remaining 2 layers on a baking sheet and spread half the ganache over each one, stopping about ½ inch from the edges. Refrigerate for about 10 minutes, or until the chocolate is set.

STEP 12 Spread a scant cup of the buttercream over the chocolate on each layer. Stack the 2 meringues, and place the reserved layer on top. Spread the remaining buttercream over the top and sides of the cake. Press some of the sliced almonds into the sides and sprinkle the rest over the top. Refrigerate for at least 2 hours, until the buttercream is thoroughly chilled and set, or for up to 12 hours.

STEP 13 To serve, dust the top of the cake with confectioners' sugar. Cut into wedges using a sawing motion with a serrated knife.

BUTTERCREAM

6	large egg yolks, at room temperature
1	cup sugar
½	cup heavy (whipping) cream
2	tablespoons instant espresso powder
¼	teaspoon salt
1 ¼	cups (2 ½ sticks) unsalted butter, cut into tablespoons, at room temperature
	Confectioners' sugar for dusting

brown butter–crème fraîche
pound cake

SERVES 8 TO 10

This pound cake is perfect in its simplicity. The nutty brown butter adds a terrific flavor and also makes for a wonderful, very dark brown crust. Don't worry if it looks as if it's getting too dark—it's always the little browned bits that taste best.

2	cups all-purpose flour
1	teaspoon baking powder
¼	teaspoon salt
1	cup (2 sticks) unsalted butter
1 ¼	cups sugar
4	large eggs, at room temperature
½	cup crème fraîche, homemade (page 12) or store-bought, or sour cream, at room temperature
2	teaspoons pure vanilla extract

STEP 1 Position a rack in the lower third of the oven and preheat the oven to 350°F. Butter and flour a 9-by-5-by-3-inch loaf pan and shake out the excess flour.

STEP 2 Sift together the 2 cups flour, the baking powder, and salt onto a sheet of wax paper.

STEP 3 Heat the butter in a medium heavy saucepan or skillet over low heat until it is a nutty brown color; watch it carefully so it doesn't burn. Immediately pour it into a large bowl.

STEP 4 Add the sugar to the butter and, with an electric mixer on medium speed, beat until the mixture cools to room temperature. Add the eggs one at a time, beating well after each addition. On low speed, add the flour mixture alternately with the crème fraîche in 3 batches, beating until just combined after each addition. Beat in the vanilla. Transfer the batter to the pan and smooth the top with a rubber spatula.

STEP 5 Bake for 1 hour and 5 to 10 minutes, or until a wooden pick inserted in the center comes out clean and the cake begins to pull away from the sides of the pan. Cool for 10 minutes in the pan on a wire rack, then turn out onto the rack and turn right side up to cool completely. Serve cut into slices.

creamy rice pudding cake

SERVES 8 TO 10

This is lovely with fresh fruit, such as sliced ripe peaches, strawberries, or mango. You might also serve it with Meringue Cream (page 141).

4	cups half-and-half
²/₃	cup Arborio or other short-grain Italian rice
½	cup packed light brown sugar
8	strips lemon zest, removed with a vegetable peeler
¾	teaspoon ground coriander
	Pinch of salt
3	large eggs, lightly beaten
1 ¼	teaspoons pure vanilla extract
⅓	cup granulated sugar
2	tablespoons water

STEP 1   Bring the half-and-half, rice, brown sugar, zest, coriander, and salt to a simmer in a medium heavy saucepan over medium heat, stirring frequently. Reduce the heat and cook at a bare simmer, stirring frequently, for 15 minutes, or until most of the liquid is absorbed. Remove the pan from the heat and let stand for 10 minutes, then discard the zest and whisk in the eggs and vanilla.

STEP 2   Meanwhile, butter an 8-by-1 ½-inch round cake pan. Heat the granulated sugar and water in a small heavy saucepan over medium heat, stirring, until the sugar is dissolved. Increase the heat to high and bring the mixture to a boil, washing down the sides of the pan with a wet pastry brush if you see any sugar crystals. Boil, without stirring, and swirling the pan toward the end to even out the color, until the caramel is a dark amber color. Pour the caramel into the prepared cake pan. Let stand until cooled and hardened.

STEP 3   Position a rack in the top third of the oven and preheat the oven to 350°F.

STEP 4   Pour the rice mixture into the cake pan and smooth the top with a rubber spatula. Bake for 35 to 40 minutes, or until the top begins to brown but the center is still slightly jiggly. Let cool completely on a wire rack.

STEP 5   Run a table knife around the edges of the pan. Invert the cake onto a plate, tap on the pan, and carefully remove the pan. Serve cut into wedges.

cheesecakes, tarts, and a **couple** of **pies**

Cheesecakes, pies, and tarts are all terrific showcases for creamy concoctions. They can range from the most chic and urbane to simple and homespun. The Coconut Cream Pie (page 66) and the Especially Delicious Banana Cream Pie (page 63) are both upscale versions of the diner-style cream pie. The coconut pie is influenced by New Orleans cuisine, and the banana cream pie, with a luscious walnut crust, is very refined, like one you'd find in a fine bakery or restaurant. I think the Cannoli Cheesecake (page 51) is even better than regular cannoli, which stuffs the filling inside a fried shell. Those fried shells are often soggy, but this cake has all those great flavors and there's nothing soggy about it. The Pumpkin Cheesecake with Gingersnap Crust (page 53) is perfect for any autumn or winter holiday or celebration. Make the Blackberry-Ripple Lime Cheesecake (page 49) in late summer or early fall, when blackberries are at their peak, and you will be thrilled by its flavor, texture, and splendid bountiful appearance. The Medieval-Style Honey and Saffron Cream Tart (page 58) is stunning in its simplicity, and the saffron is a lovely surprise. The Quebec-Style Cream and Sugar Flan (page 61) is an unusual and delicious dessert. The crust is a buttery bread dough, very easy to work with, and the filling is just cream, dark brown sugar, and walnuts, which come together to make a scrumptious combination that is starkly simple and very good to eat. Finally, the French-Style Orange Custard Tart (page 54) and the Lime Tart with Brown Butter Crust (page 55) are both refreshing treats.

blackberry-ripple
lime cheesecake

SERVES 10

Rippling the blackberry purée through the batter gives this cheesecake a gorgeous, dramatic look. It might sound difficult, but all you need to do is drizzle the purée in a spiral pattern on top of the batter, then use a table knife to swirl the purée. Don't overdo the swirling; a few quick motions will be plenty.

In this recipe, as always, I use a Microplane for zesting. It's a rasp, like one in a carpenter's tool chest, and is a great tool. Its razor-sharp teeth shave instead of ripping and shredding, and it removes a lot more zest than other gadgets.

CRUST

1 ½	cups pecans
½	cup all-purpose flour
2	tablespoons sugar
¼	cup (1/2 stick) unsalted butter, melted

FILLING

Two	6-ounce packages ripe blackberries
2	tablespoons packed light brown sugar
1	teaspoon cornstarch
1 ½	pounds cream cheese, at room temperature
One	14-ounce can sweetened condensed milk
2	teaspoons finely grated lime zest
¼	cup fresh lime juice
1	teaspoon pure vanilla extract
3	large eggs, at room temperature

STEP 1 Position a rack in the middle of the oven and preheat the oven to 350°F. Generously butter the bottom and sides of a 9-inch springform pan.

STEP 2 To make the crust: Pulse the pecans, flour, and sugar in a food processor until the nuts are finely ground. Add the butter and pulse just until combined. Press the crust evenly over the bottom and 1 inch up the sides of the pan. Bake for 10 to 12 minutes, until light brown. Transfer to a wire rack and cool completely. Reduce the oven temperature to 300°F.

STEP 3 To make the filling: Mash the blackberries and sugar together in a medium saucepan with a pastry blender or a fork. Cook over medium heat, stirring occasionally, until the berries begin to release their juices. Stir in the cornstarch, bring to a boil over medium-high heat, stirring constantly, and boil for 1 minute. Pour the purée through a coarse strainer set over a small bowl, pressing hard on the solids to extract as much liquid as possible. Refrigerate, tightly covered, until thoroughly chilled.

continued ...

blackberry-ripple lime cheesecake

... continued

STEP 4 With an electric mixer on medium-high speed, beat the cream cheese in a large bowl for about 2 minutes, until light and fluffy. Gradually beat in the condensed milk, zest, lime juice, and vanilla, scraping down the side of the bowl as necessary. Reduce the speed to medium and add the eggs one at a time, beating well after each addition. Pour the batter into the pan.

STEP 5 Transfer the blackberry purée to a small glass measure. Drizzle it in a spiral pattern over the batter, then swirl a table knife through the batter to marbleize it. Bake for 55 to 60 minutes, until the cheesecake is puffed on the sides and still slightly jiggly in the center. Let cool on a wire rack.

STEP 6 Refrigerate the cheesecake, tightly covered, for at least 8 hours, until thoroughly chilled and set, or for up to 2 days.

STEP 7 To serve, run a sharp knife around the edge of the pan to loosen the cake and remove the side of the pan. Cut the cheesecake cut into thin wedges with a sharp knife dipped into hot water and wiped dry after each cut.

cannoli cheesecake

SERVES 12

If you can get ricotta made from sheep's milk, by all means do! I get mine at the Union Square farmers' market in New York City, but there are many other places where you can pick some up. You could use chopped dried tart cherries instead of the raisins.

1	cup miniature semisweet chocolate chips
½	cup golden raisins
½	cup coarsely chopped pistachio nuts
½	cup all-purpose flour
8	large eggs
1¼	cups sugar
2	teaspoons pure vanilla extract
2	teaspoons finely grated lemon zest
1	teaspoon finely grated orange zest
¼	teaspoon salt
3	pounds whole-milk ricotta cheese

STEP 1 Position a rack in the middle of the oven and preheat the oven to 350°F. Butter and flour a 9-inch springform pan. Wrap the outside with heavy-duty aluminum foil. Have ready a roasting pan. Put on a kettle of water to boil for the water bath.

STEP 2 Toss the chocolate chips, raisins, and pistachios with the ½ cup flour in a medium bowl.

STEP 3 With an electric mixer on medium-low speed, beat the eggs, sugar, vanilla, lemon zest, orange zest, and salt in a large deep bowl just until well combined. Add the ricotta and beat, scraping down the side of the bowl as necessary, until smooth. Stir in the flour mixture with a wooden spoon until well combined.

STEP 4 Transfer the batter to the springform pan. Place the springform pan in the roasting pan and place in the oven. Carefully pour enough boiling water to come to a depth of about 1 inch into the roasting pan. Bake for 1 hour and 30 to 40 minutes, or until the top is golden brown and a knife inserted 2 inches from the center of the cake comes out clean. Turn off the oven and prop the door slightly open with a wooden spoon. Let the cake sit for 30 minutes in the turned-off oven.

STEP 5 Remove the cake from the water bath and remove the foil. Cool completely on a wire rack. Chill the cheesecake, loosely covered, for at least 12 hours, until thoroughly chilled and set, or for up to 2 days.

STEP 6 To serve, run a table knife around the edge of the pan and remove the pan side. Let the cheesecake stand at room temperature for 20 minutes. Serve cut into thin wedges with a sharp knife dipped into hot water and wiped dry after each cut.

pumpkin cheesecake with gingersnap crust

SERVES 8 TO 10

Would you rather have pumpkin pie or a luscious cheesecake for your holiday dessert? Make this, and you won't have that terribly difficult choice. Serve the cheesecake sprinkled with coarsely or finely ground Praline (page 144), if you'd like.

STEP 1 Preheat the oven to 350°F. Lightly butter an 8- or 8 ½-inch springform pan.

STEP 2 To make the crust: Stir together all of the ingredients in a medium bowl until the crumbs are moistened. Press the mixture over the bottom and up the sides of the pan. Bake the crust for 10 minutes. Let cool completely on a wire rack. Increase the oven temperature to 425°F.

STEP 3 To make the filling: With an electric mixer on medium speed, beat the cream cheese, brown sugar, and granulated sugar in a large deep bowl until light and fluffy. Beat in the eggs and then the egg yolks one at a time, beating well after each addition. Add the flour and pumpkin pie spice and beat on low speed just until combined. Add the pumpkin purée, crème fraîche, and vanilla, and beat just until combined. Pour the filling into the shell.

CRUST

1 ½	cups gingersnap cookie crumbs
½	cup finely chopped hazelnuts
6	tablespoons (¾ stick) unsalted butter, melted
¼	cup sugar

FILLING

1 ½	pounds cream cheese, at room temperature
½	cup packed light brown sugar
¼	cup granulated sugar
2	large eggs
2	large egg yolks
1 ½	tablespoons all-purpose flour
2	teaspoons pumpkin pie spice
1	cup solid-pack pumpkin purée (not pumpkin pie mix)
½	cup crème fraîche, homemade (page 12) or store-bought, or sour cream
2	teaspoons pure vanilla extract

STEP 4 Place the cheesecake on a baking sheet and bake for 15 minutes. Reduce the oven temperature to 250°F and continue baking for 1 hour.

STEP 5 Turn the oven off and let the cheesecake cool in the oven for 2 ½ hours. Then transfer to a wire rack and let cool to room temperature. Refrigerate, tightly covered, for at least 10 hours, until thoroughly chilled and set, or for up to 2 days.

STEP 6 To serve, run a knife around the side of the cheesecake and remove the side of the pan. Serve slightly chilled or at room temperature, cut into thin wedges with a sharp knife dipped into hot water and wiped dry after each cut.

french-style **orange custard** tart

SERVES 8 TO 10

If you'd like, dust the tart with confectioners' sugar and serve with fragrant ripe strawberries.

STEP 1 To make the pastry: Whisk together the flour and salt in a large bowl. With a pastry blender or 2 knives used scissors-fashion, cut in the butter until the mixture resembles small crumbs. Add the water 1 tablespoon at a time, mixing lightly with the fork after each addition, until the dough just comes together if a small bit is pressed between your fingers; do not overmix. Shape the dough into a disk, wrap in wax paper, and refrigerate for at least 30 minutes, or for up to 2 days. (If it has been chilled overnight or longer, let the dough stand at room temperature for 20 minutes before rolling it out.)

STEP 2 On a lightly floured surface, with a floured rolling pin, roll the pastry into a 14-inch round. Fold the pastry in half and transfer it to an 11-inch fluted tart pan with a removable bottom. Unfold the pastry and gently press it into the bottom and up the sides of the pan with your fingertips. Trim the overhanging pastry to 1 inch. Fold the overhang in and then press the dough against the sides of the pan so it extends about ¼ inch above the rim. Refrigerate for 15 minutes.

PASTRY

1 ½	cups all-purpose flour
½	teaspoon salt
½	cup (1 stick) plus 2 tablespoons cold unsalted butter, cut into small pieces
3 to 4	tablespoons ice water

FILLING

6	large eggs
1	cup sugar
¾	teaspoon finely grated orange zest
½	teaspoon finely grated lemon zest
¼	cup fresh orange juice
¼	cup fresh lemon juice
¼	teaspoon salt
½	cup crème fraîche, homemade (page 12) or store-bought, or heavy (whipping) cream

STEP 3 Preheat the oven to 425°F.

STEP 4 Press a piece of heavy-duty aluminum foil snugly into the bottom and up the sides of the pastry shell and fill with uncooked rice or dried beans. Bake for 15 minutes. Remove the foil and rice, and bake for 8 to 10 minutes longer, until golden brown. (If the shell puffs up during baking, gently press it down with the back of a spoon.) Let cool on a wire rack. Reduce the oven temperature to 350°F.

STEP 5 To make the filling: Whisk together the eggs, sugar, orange zest, lemon zest, orange juice, lemon juice, and salt in a medium bowl until well combined. Whisk in the crème fraîche.

STEP 6 Carefully pour the filling into the cooled tart shell. Place on a baking sheet and bake for 30 minutes, or until the edges are set but the center is still slightly jiggly. Cool completely on a wire rack.

STEP 7 To serve, remove the side of the pan and cut into wedges.

lime tart with brown butter crust

SERVES 8

You can use plain melted butter for the crust, but brown butter adds a richness that is superb. You might switch things around and use the Passion Fruit Curd (page 32) for the filling—it's excellent with the lime sugar. If you don't have a spice grinder to make the topping, serve the tart sprinkled with Lemon Crunch (page 146).

LIME CURD

½	cup (1 stick) unsalted butter
5	large egg yolks
½	cup sugar
	Finely grated zest of 1 lime
½	cup fresh lime juice
	Pinch of salt
¾	cup heavy (whipping) cream

STEP 1 To make the curd: Melt the butter in a large heavy saucepan over medium-low heat. Remove the pan from the heat and whisk in the egg yolks, sugar, lime zest, juice, and salt. Return to medium heat and cook, whisking

PASTRY

6	tablespoons (¾ stick) unsalted butter
1 ½	cups all-purpose flour
2	tablespoons sugar
¼	teaspoon salt

frequently at first and constantly toward the end, for about 10 minutes, until thickened.

STEP 2 Immediately pour the curd through a fine strainer set over a medium glass measure or bowl. Let cool to room temperature, whisking occasionally; the curd will continue to thicken as it cools. Refrigerate, tightly covered, for about 2 hours, until thoroughly chilled and set. (The curd can be refrigerated for up to 1 month.)

STEP 3 To make the pastry: Heat the butter in a small heavy saucepan or skillet over low heat until it is a nutty brown color; watch it carefully so it doesn't burn. Immediately pour the butter into a small glass measure or heatproof bowl and let cool to room temperature.

STEP 4 Position a rack in the middle of the oven and preheat the oven to 350°F.

STEP 5 Whisk together the flour, sugar, and salt in a medium bowl. Slowly pour in the butter, stirring constantly with a fork, and continue stirring just until the dough holds together when a small bit is pressed between your fingers. *continued ...*

lime tart with brown butter crust

continued ...

STEP 6 Transfer the dough to a 9-inch fluted tart pan with a removable bottom. Press the dough evenly into the bottom and up the sides of the pan. Prick all over with a fork. Bake for 20 minutes, or until light golden brown. Let cool on a wire rack.

STEP 7 With an electric mixer on medium-high speed, beat the cream in a medium bowl just until it forms stiff peaks when the beaters are lifted. Whisk in the lime curd just until combined. Transfer the filling to the crust and smooth the top with a rubber spatula. Refrigerate for at least 4 hours, until thoroughly chilled and set, or for up to 8 hours.

STEP 8 Just before serving, make the topping: Pulse the sugar and lime zest in a spice grinder until the zest is finely ground. Sprinkle evenly over the tart and serve cut into wedges.

TOPPING

2   teaspoons sugar

1   teaspoon finely grated lime zest

medieval-style **honey** and **saffron cream** tart

SERVES 8

When you taste it, you'll see why this tart has been made since the Middle Ages. Try serving it with fruit—raspberries tossed with sugar, roasted apricots or cherries, or sliced ripe figs.

Pastry crusts baked "blind," without a filling, sometimes have a tendency to crack. To remedy that, use a bit of the leftover dough scraps, or make a paste with flour and water, and patch the crust with a thin smear while it's still hot.

PASTRY

1 ²/₃	cups all-purpose flour
2	tablespoons confectioners' sugar
¼	teaspoon salt
½	cup (1 stick) cold unsalted butter, cut into small pieces
2	large egg yolks
2 to 3	tablespoons ice water

STEP 1 To make the pastry: Pulse the flour, sugar, and salt in a food processor until well combined. Add the butter and process for 30 seconds, just until the mixture resembles fine crumbs. Stir together the egg yolks and 2 tablespoons water with a fork in a small bowl. Add the yolk mixture to the flour mixture and process for 10 seconds, or just until the dough holds together when you pinch some between your fingers; if necessary, add some or all of the remaining 1 tablespoon water. Turn the dough out onto a lightly floured surface and knead gently until smooth. Shape into a disk, wrap the disk in wax paper, and refrigerate for at least 30 minutes, or for up to 1 day.

STEP 2 On a lightly floured surface, roll out the pastry to a 12-inch round. Fold the pastry in half and transfer it to a 9-inch fluted tart pan with a removable bottom. Unfold the pastry and gently press it into the bottom and up the sides of the pan with your fingertips. Trim the overhanging edge of the pastry to 1 inch. Fold the overhang in and press the pastry against the sides of the pan so it extends about ¼ inch above the rim. Prick the bottom and sides all over with a fork. Refrigerate for 30 minutes.

STEP 3 Preheat the oven to 375°F.

STEP 4 Press a piece of heavy-duty aluminum foil snugly into the bottom and up the sides of the pastry shell and fill with uncooked rice or dried beans. Bake for 15 minutes. Remove the foil and the rice, and bake for 5 minutes longer, or until lightly browned. Transfer to a wire rack. Reduce the oven temperature to 350°F.

continued ...

LUSCIOUS CREAMY DESSERTS

medieval-style honey and saffron cream tart ... *continued*

FILLING

1 ¼	cups heavy (whipping) cream
⅓	cup whole milk
3 to 4	tablespoons honey, preferably dark honey
Scant ¼	teaspoon saffron threads, crumbled
	Pinch of salt
6	large egg yolks

STEP 5 To make the filling: Bring the cream, milk, 3 tablespoons of the honey, the saffron, and salt just to a boil in a medium heavy saucepan over medium heat. Remove the pan from the heat and let steep, covered, for 15 minutes.

STEP 6 Taste the honey mixture and add the remaining 1 tablespoon honey, if desired. Whisk together the egg yolks in a medium bowl. Slowly pour in the honey mixture, whisking constantly. Pour the mixture through a fine strainer set over a medium glass measure or bowl, then pour the filling into the pastry shell.

STEP 7 Place the tart on a baking sheet and bake for 25 to 30 minutes, until set around the edges but still slightly jiggly in the center. Cool slightly on a wire rack.

STEP 8 Remove the side of the pan and serve the tart warm, cut into wedges.

quebec-style cream and sugar flan

SERVES 8 TO 10

The yeast dough makes a fantastic crust. It gets dark, like bread dough, as does the filling. If that bothers you, put strips of foil over the rim of crust when it gets dark enough for you; I like it dark. The dough is really easy to work with and to roll out. You can knead it in a stand mixer with the dough hook, if you'd like.

DOUGH

¼	cup warm water (105° to 115°F)
3	tablespoons sugar
½	teaspoon active dry yeast
1 ¾	cups all-purpose flour
	Pinch of salt
½	cup (1 stick) cold unsalted butter, cut into small pieces
1	large egg

STEP 1 To make the dough: Stir together the water, 1 tablespoon of the sugar, and the yeast in a small bowl. Let stand in a warm place for 5 to 10 minutes, or until foamy.

STEP 2 Whisk together the flour and salt in a medium bowl. Cut in the butter with a pastry blender or 2 knives used scissors-fashion until the mixture resembles coarse crumbs. Make a well in the center and add the egg, the remaining 2 tablespoons sugar, and the yeast mixture. Stir with a wooden spoon until you have a soft, slightly sticky dough. Turn out onto a work surface and knead vigorously for 10 minutes, or until smooth and elastic. Form the dough into a ball, transfer to a bowl, and refrigerate for 30 minutes.

STEP 3 Preheat the oven to 400°F. Butter a 10-inch fluted tart pan with a removable bottom.

STEP 4 On a lightly floured surface, roll out the dough to a 13-inch round. Fold the pastry in half and transfer to

continued ...

quebec-style cream and sugar flan

... continued

the tart pan. Unfold the dough and gently press it into the bottom and up the sides of the pan with your fingertips. Trim the overhanging edge of the dough to 1 inch. Fold the overhang in and press the dough against the sides of the pan so it extends about ¼ inch above the rim.

STEP 5 Press a piece of heavy-duty aluminum foil snugly into the bottom and up the sides of the pastry shell and fill with uncooked rice or dried beans. Bake for 10 minutes. Remove the foil with the rice.

STEP 6 Meanwhile, make the filling: Bring the sugar and crème fraîche to a boil in a medium saucepan over medium heat, stirring until the sugar is dissolved. Remove the pan from the heat and stir in the walnuts, lemon juice, and salt.

STEP 7 Pour the cream mixture into the crust. Place on a baking sheet and bake for 20 to 25 minutes, until the crust is dark brown and the filling is set around the edges but slightly jiggly in the center. Cool completely on a wire rack.

STEP 8 Refrigerate the tart for at least 3 hours, until thoroughly chilled and set, or for up to 1 day.

STEP 9 Remove the side of the pan and serve the flan cold, sliced into wedges.

FILLING

1 cup plus 2 tablespoons packed dark brown sugar

1 cup crème fraîche, homemade (page 12) or store-bought, or heavy (whipping) cream

1 cup walnuts, coarsely chopped

2 teaspoons fresh lemon juice

Pinch of salt

especially delicious
banana cream pie

SERVES 4

This pie is lusciously creamy and wonderful exactly as it is, but if you'd like to fancy it up, whip some extra cream and add a dollop of cream and a thin banana slice as a garnish for each serving. The dough is very easy to work with, and it patches beautifully if necessary.

PASTRY

¾	cup walnuts
¾	cup all-purpose flour
	Pinch of salt
	Pinch of baking powder
6	tablespoons (¾ stick) unsalted butter, at room temperature
¼	cup sugar
1	large egg yolk

STEP 1 To make the pastry: Preheat the oven to 350°F.

STEP 2 Spread the walnuts on a baking sheet and toast for about 12 minutes, until golden brown and fragrant. Transfer to a plate to cool completely.

STEP 3 Pulse the walnuts in a food processor until finely ground. Transfer to a medium bowl, add the flour, salt, and baking powder, and whisk together; set aside. With an electric mixer on medium-high speed, beat the butter and sugar in a large bowl until light and fluffy. Beat in the egg yolk just until combined. Whisk in the walnut mixture until well combined. Shape the dough into a disk, wrap in wax paper, and refrigerate for at least 1 hour, or for up to 1 day.

STEP 4 Roll out the dough between 2 sheets of wax paper to a 12-inch circle. Remove the top sheet of paper, invert the crust into a 9-inch pie pan, and remove the remaining wax paper. Gently ease the dough into the pan. Trim the excess dough and crimp the edges decoratively. Refrigerate for 30 minutes.

STEP 5 Preheat the oven to 350°F.

STEP 6 Press a piece of heavy-duty aluminum foil snugly into the bottom and up the sides of the pastry shell and fill with uncooked rice or dried beans. Bake for 15 minutes. Remove the foil and the rice and bake for 10 minutes longer, or until golden brown. Cool completely on a wire rack. *continued ...*

especially delicious banana
cream pie ... *continued*

FILLING

1 ½	teaspoons plain gelatin
¼	cup water
1	cup half-and-half
⅓	cup sugar
1	tablespoon cornstarch
3	large egg yolks
2	teaspoons pure vanilla extract
¾	cup heavy (whipping) cream
4	ripe bananas

Coarsely or finely ground Praline
(page 144; optional)

STEP 7 To make the filling: Sprinkle the gelatin over the water in a small bowl and let stand for 10 minutes, or until softened.

STEP 8 Meanwhile, heat the half-and-half in a medium saucepan over medium heat until hot. Whisk together the sugar and cornstarch in a medium bowl. Add the egg yolks and whisk until smooth. Slowly pour the half-and-half into the yolk mixture, whisking constantly. Return the mixture to the saucepan and bring to a boil, whisking constantly. Reduce the heat to low and cook for 2 minutes, whisking constantly. Transfer to a bowl, add the gelatin mixture, and whisk until dissolved. Whisk in the vanilla. Let cool to room temperature, whisking occasionally.

STEP 9 Refrigerate the gelatin mixture, tightly covered, for 30 to 45 minutes, or until beginning to set; when dropped from a spoon, the mixture will mound slightly.

STEP 10 With an electric mixer on medium-high speed, beat the cream in a medium bowl just until it forms stiff peaks when the beaters are lifted. With a whisk or a rubber spatula, gently fold the cream into the gelatin mixture. Peel and thinly slice the bananas, folding them into the filling as they are cut. Pour into the crust and smooth the top. Refrigerate, tightly covered, for at least 2 hours, until thoroughly chilled and set, or for up to 5 hours.

STEP 11 To serve, sprinkle the pie with the Praline, if using, and cut into wedges.

coconut cream pie
with pecan crust

SERVES 8 TO 10

This pie has the classic New Orleans combination of pecans and coconut. Want a garnish for the top? Reserve a couple tablespoons of the coconut or sprinkle with chopped pecans.

1 ¼	cups finely shredded unsweetened coconut
1	cup pecans
1	cup sugar
2	tablespoons cornstarch
2 ¾	cups heavy (whipping) cream
3	large egg yolks
½	teaspoon pure vanilla extract
½	cup all-purpose flour
¼	cup (1/2 stick) unsalted butter, at room temperature
¼	teaspoon salt

STEP 1 Preheat the oven to 350°F.

STEP 2 Spread the coconut on a large baking sheet and the pecans on another baking sheet. Toast the coconut for 5 to 7 minutes, until lightly golden, and the pecans for 10 to 12 minutes, until fragrant, stirring both halfway through. Transfer to separate plates to cool.

STEP 3 Meanwhile, stir together ½ cup of the sugar and the cornstarch with a fork in a small bowl. Whisk together ½ cup of the cream and 2 egg yolks in a medium bowl. Whisk in the sugar mixture.

STEP 4 Heat 1 ¼ cups of the cream in a medium heavy saucepan over medium heat until hot. Slowly pour the cream into the yolk mixture, whisking constantly. Return to the saucepan, reduce the heat to medium-low, and cook, whisking frequently, for 5 to 7 minutes, or until thickened. Pour through a coarse strainer set over a bowl. Whisk in the vanilla, and place a piece of plastic wrap directly on the surface of the pastry cream to keep a skin from forming. Let cool to room temperature, then refrigerate the pastry cream for about 2 hours, until thoroughly chilled and set, or for up to 1 day.

STEP 5 Pulse the pecans and flour in a food processor just until the pecans are finely ground.

STEP 6 With an electric mixer on medium-high speed, beat the butter, ¼ cup of the sugar, and the salt in a medium bowl until light and fluffy. Add the remaining egg yolk and beat until well combined. Add the pecan mixture and stir with a rubber spatula until combined. Shape the dough into a disk, wrap in wax paper, and refrigerate for at least 1 hour, until firm, or for up to 1 day.

STEP 7 Preheat the oven to 350°F.

STEP 8 Roll out the dough between 2 sheets of wax paper to a 12-inch circle. Remove the top sheet of paper, invert the crust into a 9-inch pie pan, and remove the remaining wax paper. Gently ease the dough into the pan. (The dough patches well, so don't worry if you need to press more dough into a thin place or patch a crack.) Trim the excess dough and crimp the edges decoratively.

STEP 9 Press a piece of heavy-duty aluminum foil snugly into the bottom and up the sides of the pastry shell and fill with uncooked rice or dried beans. Bake for 15 minutes. Remove the foil and rice and bake for 10 to 15 minutes longer, until golden brown. Let cool on a wire rack.

STEP 10 With an electric mixer on medium speed, beat the chilled pastry cream, the remaining 1 cup heavy cream, and the remaining ¼ cup sugar in a large deep bowl until the mixture forms soft peaks when the beaters are lifted. With a whisk or a rubber spatula, fold in the coconut. Spoon into the piecrust and swirl the top. Refrigerate for at least 2 hours, until thoroughly chilled and set, or for up to 6 hours.

STEP 11 Serve cut into wedges.

puddings and other spoonable desserts

Because I'm so crazy about this category of desserts, you have quite a choice—I couldn't resist including all my favorites. The Butterscotch Pudding (page 72) is not only creamy, it has a rich real butterscotch flavor, and what's better than butterscotch? Another cozy dessert is the very tropical Coconut Rice Pudding Parfait with Mango and Basil (page 75). The flavor combination is excellent, it's very easy to make, and the presentation is dramatic. The Tarragon Cup Custard (page 71) is both down-to-earth and exotic. Tarragon may be unusual in a dessert, but it is a real treat here—the custard has a sweet, very subtle licorice flavor. There are also several classics of French cuisine: The Luscious Crème Brûlée (page 76) is made as one large dessert, not individual servings, and looks even more beautiful and inviting that way. Pots de Crème (page 79) made with Grand Marnier are a delightful little dessert. The Coeur à la Crème (page 86) is perfectly smooth and creamy and can be served with caramel oranges, fresh berries, or whatever you choose. The Classic Crème Caramel (page 78), my favorite dessert of all, is strikingly simple. The Crème Carême (page 80), named after the famous French chef, is a charming old-fashioned and unusual dessert that will wow your friends and family. Or try the Chilled Chocolate Soufflé with Lots of Ginger (page 89)—it's splendid and sophisticated. You'll love the rich and creamy Lemon and Ginger Brioche Bread Pudding (page 87). Based on a luscious custard, it has lots of flavor and maybe the world's most comforting texture. There are two panna cottas to choose from. The Clementine Panna Cotta (page 81) is refreshing and served with a simple blueberry sauce. The Black Pepper, Bay Laurel, and Honey Panna Cotta (page 82) is modeled after an outrageously good dessert I had at Lupa, one of Mario Batali's New York City restaurants. It's earthy and sublime. And last, the classic Greek Yogurt with Sour Cherry Preserves, Walnuts, and Honey (page 84) is the perfect ending for almost any meal all year round.

tarragon cup custard

SERVES 4

You have never had a dessert flavored with an herb? Don't be afraid. The tarragon flavor in the custard is delicate and divine. This is terrific sprinkled with either crunchy pistachio nuts (page 145) or a pinch of Lemon Crunch (page 146).

For the best texture, skim any bubbles from the tops of the custards before baking them.

2	cups half-and-half
¼	cup packed light brown sugar
8	sprigs fresh tarragon, coarsely chopped
Three	1/2-inch strips lemon zest, removed with a vegetable peeler
1	teaspoon coriander seeds
6	large egg yolks
	Pinch of salt

STEP 1 Bring the half-and-half and sugar just to a boil in a medium saucepan over medium heat, whisking until the sugar is dissolved. Remove the pan from the heat and stir in the tarragon, zest, and coriander. Let stand, covered, for 15 minutes.

STEP 2 Preheat the oven to 350°F. Have ready four 6-ounce ramekins or custard cups and a 10-inch square baking pan. Put on a kettle of water to boil for the water bath.

STEP 3 Whisk together the yolks and salt in a medium bowl. Slowly pour in the half-and-half mixture, whisking constantly until blended and smooth. Pour the mixture through a fine strainer set over a medium glass measure or bowl, pressing hard on the solids to extract as much liquid as possible.

STEP 4 Divide the custard evenly among the ramekins. Skim any foam on top, transfer to the baking pan, and pour enough boiling water into the pan to reach halfway up the sides of the ramekins. Bake for about 40 minutes, or until the custard is just set around the edges but still slightly jiggly in the center; do not overbake—the custards will set further as they cool.

STEP 5 Transfer the custards to a wire rack and let cool for about 15 minutes to serve warm. Or let cool to room temperature and refrigerate, tightly covered, for up to 1 day to serve chilled.

better-than-classic
butterscotch pudding

SERVES 4

For a more adult pudding, replace a tablespoon of the milk with the same amount of Scotch whisky. You might also substitute a tablespoon or two of muscovado sugar for the dark brown sugar to add yet another dimension of flavor. My favorite garnish is a tiny dollop of crème fraîche or whipped cream with a dusting of coarsely or finely ground Praline or a shard of Praline (page 144).

1 ½	cups whole milk
2	tablespoons cornstarch
¼	cup (½ stick) unsalted butter
½	cup packed dark brown sugar
8	large egg yolks
	Pinch of salt
1	teaspoon fresh lemon juice
½	teaspoon pure vanilla extract

STEP 1 Whisk together the milk and cornstarch in a medium bowl.

STEP 2 Melt the butter in a large heavy saucepan over medium heat. Add the brown sugar and cook, whisking frequently, for 2 to 3 minutes, until the mixture is smooth and bubbling. Slowly and carefully pour in the milk mixture—it will sputter at first—whisking constantly. Cook, whisking, for about 2 minutes, until the mixture is hot and there are no lumps of sugar left. Remove the pan from the heat.

STEP 3 Whisk together the egg yolks and salt in a medium bowl. Slowly pour in the milk mixture, whisking constantly. Return the mixture to the saucepan and cook over medium-low heat, whisking constantly, for 6 to 8 minutes, or until the mixture comes to a boil and large bubbles rise to the surface.

STEP 4 Immediately pour the mixture through a fine strainer set over a medium glass measure or bowl. Whisk in the lemon juice and vanilla. Let cool for 15 minutes, whisking occasionally to keep a skin from forming.

STEP 5 Divide the pudding evenly among four 6-ounce ramekins or custard cups. Place a piece of plastic wrap directly on the surface of each pudding to keep a skin from forming. Let cool to room temperature, then refrigerate for about 3 hours, until thoroughly chilled and set, or for up to 2 days before serving.

coconut rice pudding parfait with mango and basil

SERVES 8

To finely shred the basil leaves, just stack them and cut them with a very sharp knife crosswise into the thinnest possible slivers. For garnish, you could prepare Praline (page 144) with coconut or sesame seeds and serve it on the side.

2 ½	cups water
	Pinch of salt
1	cup long-grain white rice, preferably jasmine or basmati
2	cups whole milk
One	13 1/2- to 14 1/2-ounce can coconut milk
¼	cup packed light brown sugar
¼	cup granulated sugar
14	fresh basil leaves
2	large firm but ripe mangoes, peeled, pitted, and finely chopped
2	tablespoons fresh lime juice

STEP 1 Bring the water and salt to a boil in a large heavy saucepan over high heat. Add the rice, reduce the heat to low, cover, and cook for 20 minutes. Remove the pan from the heat and let the rice stand, covered, for 10 minutes.

STEP 2 Stir the whole milk, coconut milk, brown sugar, and granulated sugar into the rice and bring the mixture just to a boil over medium heat. Reduce the heat and cook at a bare simmer, stirring frequently at first and constantly toward the end, for about 30 minutes, or until the mixture is thick and creamy and the rice is very soft. Transfer to a bowl and let cool to room temperature, stirring frequently to keep a skin from forming.

STEP 3 Refrigerate the rice pudding, tightly covered, for at least 4 hours, until thoroughly chilled and set, or overnight.

STEP 4 To serve, cut 6 of the basil leaves into fine shreds. Stir together the mango, shredded basil, and lime juice in a medium bowl. Spoon a layer of ½ cup rice pudding into each of 8 short glasses. Add 2 tablespoons of the mango mixture to each, top with a generous ¼ cup pudding, and add another 2 tablespoons of the mango mixture. Garnish each serving with a whole basil leaf.

luscious crème brûlée

SERVES 8

Crème brûlée is the ultimate dessert. Have you ever met anyone who didn't like it? This one is unfussy and served as one large custard, rather than in tiny ramekins. Serve yourself and enjoy.

2	cups heavy (whipping) cream
1	cup half-and-half
6	large egg yolks
¾	cup sugar
	Pinch of salt
2	teaspoons pure vanilla extract

STEP 1 Preheat the oven to 300°F. Have ready a flame-proof 1-quart shallow baking or gratin dish and a roasting pan. Put on a kettle of water to boil for the water bath.

STEP 2 Heat the cream and half-and-half in a medium saucepan over medium heat until hot. Remove from the heat.

STEP 3 Whisk together the yolks, ½ cup of the sugar, and the salt in a medium bowl. Slowly add the cream mixture, whisking constantly until blended and smooth. Add the vanilla. Pour the mixture through a fine strainer set over a medium glass measure or bowl.

STEP 4 Pour the custard into the baking dish and skim any foam from the top. Transfer to the roasting pan, place in the oven, and pour enough boiling water into the pan to reach halfway up the sides of the baking dish. Bake for 25 to 30 minutes, or until the custard is set around the edges but still slightly jiggly in the center. Do not over-bake—the custard will set further as it cools. Remove the baking dish from the water bath and let cool completely on a wire rack.

STEP 5 Refrigerate the crème brûlée, loosely covered, for at least 4 hours, until thoroughly chilled and set, or for up to 1 day.

STEP 6 Preheat the broiler. Have the roasting pan ready, and fill a bowl with ice water. Gently blot the surface of the custard with the edge of a paper towel to remove any condensation. Sift the remaining ¼ cup sugar evenly over the custard. Place the baking dish in the roasting pan and carefully pour enough ice water into the pan to come halfway up the sides of the baking dish.

STEP 7 Broil the custard about 3 inches from the heat for 2 to 3 minutes, until the sugar has melted and turned a dark amber color; carefully move or rotate the dish if necessary so the sugar caramelizes evenly. Remove from the broiler and cool the custard in the ice water for 5 minutes.

STEP 8 Carefully remove the baking dish from the baking pan. Serve right away, or refrigerate, uncovered, for no longer than 1 hour before serving—or the topping will soften.

classic **crème caramel**

SERVES 4

This may be *the* classic French dessert. It is perfectly smooth and creamy, and the sweet flavor of the custard is balanced flawlessly by the bittersweet caramel.

½	cup plus 2 tablespoons sugar
¼	cup water
1 ¼	cups half-and-half
4	large egg yolks
	Pinch of salt
½	teaspoon pure vanilla extract

STEP 1   Preheat the oven to 325°F. Have ready four 6-ounce ramekins or custard cups and a 10-inch square baking pan. Put on a kettle of water to boil for the water bath.

STEP 2   Heat ½ cup sugar and the water in a medium heavy saucepan over medium heat, stirring, until the sugar is dissolved. Increase the heat to high and bring the mixture to a boil, washing down the sides of the pan with a wet pastry brush if you see any sugar crystals. Boil, without stirring, swirling the pan toward the end to even out the color, until the caramel is a dark amber color. Immediately pour the caramel into the ramekins, tilting to coat the bottom and sides evenly. Let cool and harden at room temperature.

STEP 3   Meanwhile, heat the half-and-half in a medium saucepan over medium heat until hot. Whisk together the egg yolks, the remaining 2 tablespoons sugar, and the salt in a medium bowl. Slowly pour in the hot half-and-half, whisking constantly. Pour the custard through a fine strainer set over a medium glass measure or bowl. Whisk in the vanilla.

STEP 4   Divide the custard evenly among the ramekins. Place the ramekins in the baking pan, place it in the oven, and carefully pour enough boiling water into the pan to reach halfway up the sides of the ramekins. Bake for 35 to 40 minutes, until the custard is set around the edges but still slightly jiggly in the center; do not overbake—the custards will set further as they cool.

STEP 5   With tongs or a wide metal spatula, carefully transfer the ramekins to a wire rack and let cool to room temperature. Refrigerate, tightly covered, for at least 3 hours, until thoroughly chilled and set, or for up to 1 day.

STEP 6   To serve, run a table knife around the edges of the ramekins and invert onto serving plates.

grand marnier
pots de crème

SERVES 4

If you caramelize sugar on the top of these, just as you do for the Crème Brûlée on page 76, they will magically turn into Grand Marnier crème brûlée (just as any pots de crème would).

1	cup heavy (whipping) cream
¼	cup crème fraîche, homemade (page 12) or store-bought, or additional heavy (whipping) cream
	Pinch of salt
4	large egg yolks
2	tablespoons sugar
1	tablespoon plus 1 teaspoon Grand Marnier or other orange liqueur

STEP 1 Position a rack in the middle of the oven and preheat the oven to 300°F. Have ready four 6-ounce ramekins or custard cups and a 10-inch square baking pan. Put on a kettle of water to boil for the water bath.

STEP 2 Combine the cream, crème fraîche, and salt in a medium heavy saucepan and cook over medium heat, whisking occasionally, just until hot. Remove from the heat.

STEP 3 Whisk together the egg yolks, sugar, and Grand Marnier in a medium bowl. Slowly pour in the cream mixture, whisking constantly. Pour the mixture through a fine strainer set over a large glass measure or bowl.

STEP 4 Divide the custard evenly among the ramekins. Skim any foam from the top of the custards. Place the ramekins in the baking pan, place the pan in the oven, and carefully add enough boiling water to the baking pan to come halfway up the sides of the ramekins. Bake for 25 to 30 minutes, until the custards are set around the edges but still slightly jiggly in the center; do not overbake—the custards will set further as they cool. Remove the pan from the oven and let the custards stand in the water bath for 10 minutes.

STEP 5 With tongs or a wide metal spatula, carefully transfer the ramekins to a wire rack and let cool to room temperature. Refrigerate, tightly covered, for at least 3 hours, until thoroughly chilled and set, or for up to 2 days.

STEP 6 Serve the pots de crème chilled in the ramekins.

crème carême

SERVES 6 TO 8

This is indeed a timeless dessert, old-fashioned in the most pleasant way. My version is adapted from recipes from nineteenth-century chef Antonin Carême, Alice B. Toklas, and the *Time-Life* series volume of classic desserts. Maraschino liqueur was traditionally used, but not many of us have it in our cupboards today. I use Grand Marnier because I love it, but you could use whatever flavor you'd like. Limoncello would also be terrific. The crème is a loose, luscious foamy custard, not at all dense or firmly set. Don't make it more than eight or so hours ahead— although its flavor will still be fine, it will lose volume. You might want to serve this cloud-soft dessert in stemmed glasses. And instead of the praline, you could garnish it with the Caramel-Coated Strawberries (page 148).

3	cups half-and-half
8	large egg yolks
¾	cup sugar
2	tablespoons cornstarch
	Pinch of salt
1	teaspoon pure vanilla extract
1	cup heavy (whipping) cream
3	tablespoons Grand Marnier or other liqueur
	Coarsely or finely ground Praline (page 144) for dusting (optional)

STEP 1 Heat the half-and-half in a large heavy saucepan over medium heat until hot. Remove the pan from the heat.

STEP 2 With an electric mixer on medium-high speed, beat the egg yolks, sugar, cornstarch, and salt in a large deep bowl, scraping down the sides of the bowl with a rubber spatula as necessary, for 5 minutes, or until the mixture is very thick and pale and the volume increases by at least 3 times. Reduce the speed to low and slowly pour in the half-and-half. Return the mixture to the saucepan and cook, whisking frequently, over medium-low heat, for 8 to 10 minutes, just until the mixture is thickened and coats the back of a spoon and large bubbles rise to the surface.

STEP 3 Immediately pour the custard through a fine strainer set over a large glass measure or bowl. Let cool to room temperature, whisking frequently to keep a skin from forming. Refrigerate, tightly covered, for about 4 hours, until thoroughly chilled, or for up to 8 hours.

STEP 4 Right before serving, with an electric mixer on medium-high heat, whip the cream in a medium bowl just until stiff peaks form when the beaters are lifted. With a whisk or a rubber spatula, fold the Grand Marnier into the cream, then fold the cream into the custard.

STEP 5 Transfer the custard to bowls or stemmed glasses. Sprinkle with the praline, if using.

clementine panna cotta with blueberry sauce

SERVES 4

Those terrific boxes of clementines, with their fantastic sweet flavor, don't stay around the house for long when they're being eaten out of hand. The next time you bring some home, reserve a couple for this refreshing dessert.

1 ¾	cups heavy (whipping) cream
2	teaspoons plain gelatin
3	tablespoons sugar
2	tablespoons finely grated clementine zest
	Pinch of salt
3	tablespoons fresh clementine juice
	Blueberry Sauce (recipe follows)

STEP 1 Oil four 6-ounce ramekins or custard cups with flavorless vegetable oil.

STEP 2 Pour ¼ cup of the cream into a small bowl and sprinkle with the gelatin. Let stand for 10 minutes, or until softened. Place the bowl in a larger bowl of hot water and stir until the gelatin dissolves and the mixture is clear.

STEP 3 Meanwhile, bring the remaining 1 ½ cups cream, the sugar, zest, and salt just to a boil in a medium saucepan over medium heat. Reduce the heat to low and cook at a bare simmer for 5 minutes, stirring frequently.

STEP 4 Remove the pan from the heat and stir in the gelatin mixture and clementine juice. Pour through a fine strainer set over a medium glass measure or bowl. Divide the cream mixture evenly among the ramekins. Let cool to room temperature, then refrigerate, loosely covered, for at least 3 hours, until thoroughly chilled and set, or for up to 1 day.

STEP 5 Just before serving, dip the ramekins, one at a time, into a bowl of hot water for about 5 seconds, then run a table knife around edges and invert onto serving plates. Spoon the blueberry sauce around the panna cotta.

BLUEBERRY SAUCE
(MAKES ¾ CUP)

1	cup fresh or thawed frozen blueberries
1	tablespoon confectioners' sugar
1	tablespoon water
1	teaspoon fresh lemon juice

Combine the blueberries, sugar, and water in a medium saucepan and cook over medium heat, stirring, for 5 minutes (a little longer if using frozen berries) or until the blueberries have softened and a sauce forms. Stir in the lemon juice. Serve warm, at room temperature, or chilled. The sauce can be refrigerated, tightly covered, for up to 1 week.

black pepper, bay laurel, and
honey panna cotta

SERVES 4

This is loosely adapted from an ancient Roman custard, one Apicius wrote of roughly two thousand years ago in *De Re Coquinaria*, and a dessert I had at Lupa restaurant in New York City. Don't be afraid of the pepper—it doesn't scream pepper, but it does offer a lovely warmth in the mouth. Use your favorite honey, dark or light, and add the Balsamic and Brown Sugar Drizzle only if you feel like it.

1 ½	cups heavy (whipping) cream
1 ½	teaspoons plain gelatin
2	tablespoons honey
2	tablespoons sugar
3	small imported bay leaves or 1 large California bay leaf
1	teaspoon whole black peppercorns
	Pinch of salt
¼	cup mascarpone cheese or heavy (whipping) cream
¼	teaspoon pure vanilla extract
	Balsamic and Brown Sugar Drizzle (facing page; optional)

STEP 1 Oil four 6-ounce ramekins or custard cups with flavorless vegetable oil.

STEP 2 Pour ¼ cup of the cream into a small bowl and sprinkle with the gelatin. Let stand for 10 minutes, or until softened. Place the bowl in a larger bowl of hot water and stir until the gelatin has dissolved and the liquid is clear.

STEP 3 Meanwhile, bring the remaining 1 ¼ cups cream, the honey, sugar, bay leaves, peppercorns, and salt just to a boil in a medium saucepan over medium heat, whisking until the sugar is dissolved. Remove the pan from the heat and let stand, covered, for 10 minutes.

STEP 4 Whisk the mascarpone into the cream mixture and cook over medium-low heat, whisking frequently, for about 2 minutes, until heated through and smooth. Remove the pan from the heat, add the gelatin mixture, and whisk until smooth. Whisk in the vanilla.

STEP 5 Pour the mixture through a fine strainer set over a medium glass measure or bowl. Divide evenly among the ramekins. Let cool to room temperature, then refrigerate, tightly covered, for at least 3 hours, until thoroughly chilled and set, or for up to 1 day.

STEP 6 To serve, dip the ramekins, one at a time, into a bowl of hot water for about 5 seconds, then run a table knife around the edges and invert the panna cottas onto chilled serving plates. Spoon about ½ teaspoon of the balsamic and brown sugar drizzle over each serving, if using, and serve immediately.

optional

BALSAMIC AND BROWN SUGAR DRIZZLE

1   tablespoon packed dark brown sugar

2   teaspoons balsamic vinegar

Heat the brown sugar and vinegar in a small saucepan over low heat, stirring, until the sugar is dissolved. Cool to room temperature before serving.

greek yogurt with sour cherry preserves, walnuts, and honey

SERVES 4

Greek yogurt is widely available these days, and what a treat it is, so creamy, thick, and rich. Because this dessert is so simple, each of its ingredients should be impeccable, especially the walnuts—use the freshest you can find. This is also amazing with a bit of crushed Praline (page 144) dusting the top instead of the walnuts, or with both. I could eat this every night for a very long time. There's a stunning purity to it, and it has great flavors and textures.

20	walnut halves
1	pint thick Greek yogurt
½	cup sour cherry preserves
4	teaspoons honey, preferably thyme honey

STEP 1 Preheat the oven to 350°F.

STEP 2 Spread the walnuts on a small baking sheet and toast for about 12 minutes, or until light golden brown and fragrant. Transfer to a plate to cool.

STEP 3 Spoon the yogurt into shallow serving bowls or onto dessert plates. Top with the cherry preserves, drizzle with the honey, and top with the walnuts. Serve immediately.

coeur à la crème with caramel oranges

SERVES 4

This classic is most often served in summertime with mixed fresh berries, a berry or fruit sauce, or ripe fig or apricot halves. During the cold-weather months, the juicy orange segments tossed with caramel are great, but if you'd rather, just toss the oranges with a little orange flower water.

8	ounces cream cheese, at room temperature
1	cup crème fraîche, homemade (page 12) or store-bought, or sour cream
¼	cup confectioners' sugar
1	teaspoon fresh lemon juice
½	teaspoon pure vanilla extract
	Pinch of salt

COOK'S NOTE If you don't have the special molds, trim four 12-ounce paper cups to 3 inches high. With a small bamboo skewer, poke about 10 holes in the bottom of each cup. Line the cups with the dampened cheesecloth and proceed with the recipe.

CARAMEL ORANGES

3	large navel oranges
3–4	tablespoons Caramel Syrup (page 138)
	Pinch of salt

STEP 1 With an electric mixer on medium speed, beat together the cream cheese, crème fraîche, confectioners' sugar, lemon juice, vanilla, and salt in a medium bowl, scraping down the sides of the bowl as necessary, for about 4 minutes, until very smooth. Press through a fine strainer set over a medium bowl to remove any lumps.

STEP 2 Cut four 8-by-6-inch pieces of cheesecloth. Rinse with cold water and wring dry. Line four 3-inch heart-shaped coeur à la crème molds with the cheesecloth, letting it hang over the sides. Divide the cream cheese mixture evenly among the molds, using about ½ cup for each mold, and smooth the tops. Fold the overhanging cheesecloth over the tops, pressing it lightly. Place the molds in a shallow baking dish to catch the drips and refrigerate for at least 4 hours, or for up to 2 days.

STEP 3 To make the caramel oranges: With a sharp knife, following the curve of the fruits, remove the peel and white pith from the oranges. Cut the oranges into ½-inch dice. Transfer to a bowl and let stand for 10 minutes, then drain off the juice. Stir in 3 tablespoons caramel syrup and the salt. Taste and add the remaining tablespoon of caramel syrup, if desired.

STEP 4 Unmold the coeurs onto serving plates and carefully remove the cheesecloth. Let stand at room temperature for 10 minutes before serving. Spoon the oranges next to the hearts.

lemon and ginger
brioche bread pudding

SERVES 4 TO 6

You can serve this with a tiny drizzle of Caramel Sauce (page 135) or Caramel Mascarpone Cream (page 136). You don't need a lot of either, but you might pass more at the table, if you want to make your friends very happy. Lemon Crunch (page 146) is also a fabulous garnish. I use Del Monte's Pacific-style dried apricots, which have a wonderful balance of sweet and tart.

6	cups ½-inch cubes (with crust) brioche or other egg bread
¼	cup (½ stick) unsalted butter, melted
½	cup plus 1 tablespoon sugar
4	cups half-and-half
6	strips lemon zest, removed with a vegetable peeler
2	tablespoons minced crystallized ginger
6	large eggs
	Pinch of salt
1	teaspoon pure vanilla extract or paste
½	cup thinly sliced dried apricots, preferably Del Monte Pacific-style

STEP 1 Position a rack in the middle of the oven and preheat the oven to 350°F. Butter an 8-inch square glass baking dish.

STEP 2 Place the bread on a large baking sheet. Drizzle with the butter. Sprinkle with the 1 tablespoon sugar, and toss to coat. Spread the bread in a single layer and bake, stirring halfway through, for 15 minutes, or until a deep golden brown. Let cool on the baking sheet.

STEP 3 Meanwhile, bring the half-and-half just to a boil in a large heavy saucepan over medium-high heat. Remove the pan from the heat, stir in the zest and ginger, and let stand, covered, for 20 minutes.

STEP 4 Pour the half-and-half through a fine strainer set over a large glass measure or bowl, and wipe out the saucepan. Whisk together the eggs, the remaining ½ cup sugar, and the salt in a medium bowl. Slowly pour in the warm half-and-half, whisking constantly. Return to the saucepan and cook, whisking constantly, over medium-low heat for 5 to 7 minutes, until the custard has thickened and coats the back of a spoon; if you draw your finger across it, it should leave a track. Do not let the custard boil or scorch on the bottom; if tiny bubbles appear around the edges, remove the pan from the heat for a few minutes to cool the custard, continuing to whisk. Remove from the heat and whisk in the vanilla. Pour the mixture through a fine strainer set over a large glass measure or bowl.

STEP 5 Transfer the bread to the baking dish and toss with the apricots. Pour the custard over the bread. Push down the bread with a spoon to submerge it. Let stand for 30 minutes, or until the bread is softened.

STEP 6 Preheat the oven to 300°F. Have ready a roasting pan. Put on a kettle of water to boil for the water bath.

continued …

lemon and ginger brioche bread pudding
... continued

STEP 7 Cover the baking dish with aluminum foil and seal the edges tightly. Place the baking dish in the roasting pan and place in the oven. Pour in enough boiling water into the pan to come halfway up the sides of the baking dish. Bake for 1 hour. Carefully remove the foil and bake the bread pudding for 15 minutes longer, or until the top is golden brown but the center is still slightly jiggly. Carefully remove the baking dish from the pan and let cool slightly on a wire rack.

STEP 8 Serve the pudding warm in bowls.

chilled chocolate soufflé with lots of ginger

SERVES 4 TO 6

This cold soufflé has a deep, dark, rich chocolate flavor, and the ginger adds a thrill. Serve with a dollop of Meringue Cream (page 141) and ripe fresh berries, if you like.

½	cup water
One	¼-ounce envelope plain gelatin
1	pound bittersweet or semisweet chocolate, chopped
½	cup (1 stick) unsalted butter, cut into small pieces
¼	cup unsweetened cocoa powder
2	tablespoons brandy
6	large eggs, separated
¾	cup sugar
	Pinch of salt
3	large egg whites
½	cup finely chopped crystallized ginger
½	cup heavy (whipping) cream
1	teaspoon pure vanilla extract

STEP 1 Wrap a long folded strip of heavy-duty aluminum foil or parchment paper around a 5-cup soufflé dish to form a collar that extends about 3 inches above the rim of the dish, and secure it with tape or string. Lightly oil the dish and the inside of the foil. Refrigerate the dish until ready to use.

STEP 2 Pour ¼ cup of the water into a small bowl and sprinkle with the gelatin. Let stand for 10 minutes, or until softened.

STEP 3 Place the bowl with the gelatin in a larger bowl of hot water and stir until the gelatin has dissolved and the liquid is clear.

STEP 4 Melt the chocolate and butter with the cocoa in a heatproof bowl set over a saucepan of about 1 ½ inches of barely simmering water, whisking occasionally until smooth. Remove the bowl from the saucepan and whisk in the remaining ¼ cup water and the brandy.

STEP 5 With a handheld electric mixer on medium-high speed, beat the egg yolks, ½ cup of the sugar, and the salt in a large deep heatproof bowl until well combined. Set the bowl over the saucepan of barely simmering water and beat for 15 minutes, or until the mixture is very thick and pale. Beat in the chocolate mixture just until combined. Remove the bowl from the heat, add the gelatin mixture, and beat until the mixture cools to room temperature.

STEP 6 With clean beaters, on medium speed, beat the 9 egg whites in a large deep clean bowl until the whites form soft peaks when the beaters are lifted. Increase the heat to medium-high and sprinkle in the remaining ¼ cup sugar about 1 tablespoon at a time, beating well after each addition, then beat until the whites form stiff peaks. Beat in the ginger. *continued ...*

89 • PUDDINGS AND OTHER SPOONABLE DESSERTS

chilled chocolate souffle with lots
of ginger ... *continued*

STEP 7 With clean beaters, beat the heavy cream and vanilla on high speed in a medium bowl just until the cream forms stiff peaks.

STEP 8 Place the bowl of egg yolk mixture in a larger bowl of ice water and whisk just until it begins to thicken and set. With a whisk, gently fold in the whipped cream, and then the egg whites. Pour into the soufflé dish and smooth the top with a rubber spatula. Refrigerate for at least 4 hours, until thoroughly chilled and set, or for up to 24 hours.

STEP 9 To serve, remove the collar from the soufflé. Present the soufflé at the table and spoon onto dessert plates.

creamy frozen desserts

There are so many good ice creams for sale in the shops today that a recipe has to be very special for us to go to the trouble of making one at home. So, here are a dozen outstanding and unusual creamy frozen desserts for you. I love all of them. Perhaps my favorite is the Intensely Licorice Ice Cream (page 99). I am a big fan of good licorice, and this recipe is a knock-the-back-of-your-head-off example of a concentrated, forceful, and, dare I say, passionately flavored dessert. Anyone who loves licorice will adore it. The Exquisite Green Tea Ice Cream (page 96) is a stunning color, the new green of spring; its flavor is grassy in the very best way, and it has a sophisticated and exotic flavor. I've always thought the best ice cream in the world is prune and Armagnac, and this one (page 101) is just as good as the many I've had in the Dordogne region of France. One of my favorite Roman treats is a midmorning snack from Tazzo d'Oro, espresso granita with cream (page 109). They hand a bit of paradise across the counter in a plastic cup— a lavish dollop of unsweetened cream in the bottom and a big serving of intensely flavored espresso granita on top. Want to feel as though you've been transported to Thailand? Try the Coconut Ice Cream with Lemongrass and Kaffir Lime Leaves (page 102), and it will warm you right up. The toasted coconut provides the quintessential tropical flavor, and the lemongrass and lime leaves add very refreshing elements. Do try the Mango Kulfi (page 110). Kulfi is a style of frozen dessert from South Asia, made from a mixture that is simply too rich to churn but freezes beautifully. I love lemons, and I love meringue, and I love them frozen together. The Lemon Meringue Ice Cream (page 104) is like having your pie and ice cream, too.

You'll adore the Roasted Banana Ice Cream with Pecan Praline (page 98). The crunchy pecan praline is a great foil for the sweet creaminess of the roasted bananas. While the idea may not appeal to you immediately, I'll bet the Goat's Milk Vanilla Ice Cream (page 100) will become one of your favorites, especially if you serve it with roasted cherries and apricots. Delicate and smooth, the Toasted Almond Ice Cream with Crunchy Almonds (page 95) is a real treat. It is subtle yet full of flavor, and it is very, very good. And then there is the Caramelized Honey Ice Cream with Rosemary and Orange (page 106). The rosemary and orange add lovely herbal and refreshing citrus notes.

quick chill

In a hurry? Simply put your ice cream mixture in a large glass measure or a deep bowl, place it in a large shorter bowl, and add ice and water to the larger bowl. Stir or whisk the ice cream mixture occasionally, adding more ice to the water as it melts, until it is chilled (just make sure no ice gets in the mixture). You can use this technique for any liquid that needs to be chilled, and it will truly save you some time.

toasted almond **ice cream** with crunchy almonds

SERVES 4 TO 6

You can use blanched or unblanched almonds, but I think you get a better flavor and color with unblanched. You might serve this with Butterscotch Sauce (page 139).

2	cups whole almonds, coarsely chopped
4	cups half-and-half
6	large egg yolks
½	cup sugar
	Pinch of salt
½	cup Crunchy Nuts (page 145), made with blanched whole almonds and ¼ teaspoon salt

STEP 1 Preheat the oven to 350°F.

STEP 2 Spread the chopped almonds on a large baking sheet and toast for 15 minutes, or until golden brown and fragrant.

STEP 3 Transfer the toasted almonds to a large heavy saucepan, add the half-and-half, and bring to a boil over medium heat. Remove the pan from the heat and let stand, covered, for 45 minutes.

STEP 4 Pour the half-and-half through a coarse strainer set over a large glass measure or bowl, pressing hard on the solids to extract as much liquid as possible; discard the almonds. Set the saucepan aside.

STEP 5 Whisk together the egg yolks, sugar, and salt in a medium bowl. Slowly pour in the warm half-and-half, whisking constantly. Return to the saucepan and cook, whisking constantly, over medium-low heat until the custard has thickened and coats the back of a spoon; if you draw your finger across it, it should leave a track. Do not let the custard boil or scorch on the bottom; if tiny bubbles appear around the edges, remove the pan from the heat for a few minutes to cool the custard, continuing to whisk.

STEP 6 Pour the custard through a coarse strainer set over a large glass measure or bowl. Let cool, whisking occasionally, then refrigerate, tightly covered, for 3 hours, or until thoroughly chilled, or for up to 1 day.

STEP 7 When ready to freeze, pour the custard mixture into an ice-cream maker and freeze according to the manufacturer's instructions. Transfer to a freezer container and stir in the crunchy nuts. Freeze for at least 2 hours before serving.

STEP 8 To serve, spoon the ice cream into serving bowls or glasses.

exquisite **green tea** ice cream

SERVES 4 TO 6

Matcha is powdered Japanese ceremonial green tea. It is a gorgeous color and has a fresh green flavor and a lovely bitter sweetness. It's subtle, yet it's not. Certainly not for everyone, but this ice cream is a rare and wonderful treat when you make it with high-quality tea. Just make sure to get really good green ceremonial tea powder, not regular green tea leaves. I get my tea from Takashimaya on Fifth Avenue in New York City, but there are many other sources; try the Internet if you don't have a nearby supply. A tiny drizzle of Chocolate Sauce (page 140) sets this off perfectly, as does a tiny pinch of the tea sifted over each serving just before serving.

3 cups half-and-half

4 teaspoons *matcha* (powdered Japanese ceremonial green tea)

8 large egg yolks

½ cup packed light brown sugar

Pinch of salt

STEP 1 Heat the half-and-half in a medium saucepan over medium-high heat just until hot. Remove the saucepan from the heat, transfer ¼ cup of the half-and-half to a small bowl, and add the *matcha*. Whisk until the tea powder is dissolved.

STEP 2 Whisk together the egg yolks, sugar, and salt in a medium bowl. Slowly pour in the remaining hot half-and-half and then the *matcha* mixture, whisking constantly. Return to the saucepan and cook, whisking constantly, over medium-low heat until the custard has thickened and coats the back of a spoon; if you draw your finger across it, it should leave a track. Do not let the custard boil or scorch on the bottom; if tiny bubbles appear around the edges, remove the pan from the heat for a few minutes to cool the custard, continuing to whisk.

STEP 3 Pour the custard through a fine strainer set over a large glass measure or bowl. Let cool to room temperature, whisking occasionally, then refrigerate, tightly covered, for 3 hours, or until thoroughly chilled, or for up to 1 day.

STEP 4 When ready to freeze, pour the custard mixture into an ice-cream maker and freeze according to the manufacturer's instructions. Transfer to a freezer container and freeze for at least 2 hours before serving.

STEP 5 To serve, spoon the ice cream into serving bowls or stemmed glasses.

roasted banana ice cream with pecan praline

SERVES 4 TO 6

You might very much enjoy adding chunks of bittersweet chocolate along with the praline. Either way, you could serve the ice cream with Chocolate Sauce (page 140). The pieces of praline will be irregular; the size given in the ingredient list is just a guideline. Use whatever praline you want—pecan, peanut, or walnut.

2	ripe medium bananas, not peeled
3	cups half-and-half
6	large egg yolks
½	cup packed dark brown sugar
	Pinch of salt
1	teaspoon pure vanilla extract
¾	cup ½-inch pieces pecan Praline (page 144)
	Caramel Sauce (page 135; optional)

STEP 1 Preheat the oven to 350°F.

STEP 2 With a paring knife, pierce each banana 5 times, so they will not burst. Place the bananas on a baking sheet and roast for 45 minutes. Let cool slightly.

STEP 3 When the bananas are cool enough to handle, cut a lengthwise slit in each one, remove any strings, and transfer the pulp to a medium heavy saucepan. Mash the bananas with a fork, then add the half-and-half and cook over medium heat until hot, continuing to mash the bananas until smooth. Remove from the heat.

STEP 4 Whisk together the egg yolks, sugar, and salt in a medium bowl. Slowly pour in the hot half-and-half mixture, whisking constantly. Return to the saucepan and cook, whisking constantly, over medium-low heat until the custard has thickened and coats the back of a spoon; if you draw your finger across it, it should leave a track. Do not let the custard boil or scorch on the bottom; if tiny bubbles appear around the edges, remove the pan from the heat for a few minutes to cool the custard, continuing to whisk.

STEP 5 Pour the custard through a coarse strainer set over a large glass measure or bowl, pressing hard on the solids to extract as much liquid as possible. Stir in the vanilla. Let cool to room temperature, whisking occasionally, then refrigerate, tightly covered, for 3 hours, or until thoroughly chilled, or for up to 1 day.

STEP 6 When ready to freeze, pour the custard mixture into an ice-cream maker and freeze according to the manufacturer's instructions. Transfer to a freezer container and stir in the praline. Freeze for at least 2 hours before serving.

STEP 7 To serve, spoon the ice cream into serving bowls or glasses and top with caramel sauce, if using.

intensely **licorice** ice cream

SERVES 4 TO 6

Don't worry—although the mix for this ice cream is a rather hideous greenish gray, after you freeze it, it looks like a dark caramel ice cream. So the flavor is not only intense, it can also be a surprise. This is wonderful served in small bowls with a cup of hot espresso poured over each serving, a concoction that is called *affogato*—literally, drowned—in Italy. I use good-quality Dutch licorice for this; if that isn't available, use Panda. If you're buying Dutch licorice, look for the words *zoet*, which means sweet, and *zacht*, which means soft.

2	cups heavy (whipping) cream
2	cups half-and-half
6	ounces soft sweet licorice candy
6	large egg yolks
¼	cup packed dark brown sugar
	Pinch of salt

STEP 1 Bring the cream, half-and-half, and licorice just to a boil in a large heavy saucepan over medium heat. Reduce the heat to low and cook at a bare simmer, stirring occasionally, for about 15 minutes, until most of the licorice is dissolved. Remove the pan from the heat and let stand, covered, for 15 minutes, or until all of the licorice is dissolved.

STEP 2 Whisk together the egg yolks, sugar, and salt in a medium bowl. Slowly pour in the hot cream mixture, whisking constantly. Return to the saucepan and cook, whisking constantly, over medium-low heat until the custard has thickened and coats the back of a spoon; if you draw your finger across it, it should leave a track. Do not let the custard boil or scorch on the bottom; if tiny bubbles appear around the edges, remove the pan from the heat for a few minutes to cool the custard, continuing to whisk.

STEP 3 Pour the custard through a fine strainer set over a large glass measure or bowl. Let cool to room temperature, whisking occasionally, then refrigerate, tightly covered, for 3 hours, or until thoroughly chilled, or for up to 1 day.

STEP 4 Pour the custard mixture into an ice-cream maker and freeze according to the manufacturer's instructions. Transfer to a freezer container and freeze for at least 2 hours before serving.

STEP 5 To serve, spoon the ice cream into serving bowls or glasses.

goat's milk vanilla ice cream

SERVES 6 TO 8

If you are a fan of goat cheese, give this a try. You don't get the goat's milk flavor at first, it takes a few seconds to come on, but when it does, it is sophisticated and balances the sweetness of the ice cream perfectly. Serve this with Cajeta (page 18) or with fresh cherries, nectarines, plums, or chopped tangerines. Goat's milk is available at ethnic grocers and some supermarkets.

3	cups well-stirred goat's milk
1	cup heavy (whipping) cream
6	large egg yolks
½	cup packed light brown sugar
	Pinch of salt
½	teaspoon pure vanilla extract

STEP 1 Heat the goat's milk and cream in a large saucepan over medium heat just until hot.

STEP 2 Whisk together the egg yolks, sugar, and salt in a medium bowl. Slowly pour in the goat's milk mixture, whisking constantly. Return to the saucepan and cook, whisking constantly, over medium-low heat until the custard has thickened and coats the back of a spoon; if you draw your finger across it, it should leave a track. Do not let the custard boil or scorch on the bottom; if tiny bubbles appear around the edges, remove the pan from the heat for a few minutes to cool the custard, continuing to whisk.

STEP 3 Pour the custard through a fine strainer set over a large glass measure or bowl. Whisk in the vanilla. Let cool to room temperature, whisking occasionally, then refrigerate, tightly covered, for 3 hours, or until thoroughly chilled, or for up to 1 day.

STEP 4 When ready to freeze, pour the custard into an ice-cream maker and freeze according to the manufacturer's instructions. Transfer to a freezer container and freeze for at least 2 hours before serving.

STEP 5 To serve, spoon the ice cream into serving bowls or glasses.

prune and armagnac ice cream

SERVES 4 TO 6

Once, on a trip to California, I ate some very ripe prune plums right off the tree, each one warmed by the hot midday sun, and I won't ever forget them. They were totally ripe, amazingly flavorful, and sweeter than sugar. They were also on their way to a drying facility to become prunes. I thought I would probably never again enjoy such a treat from the tree, and about how many people will never have the chance—fortunately, good prunes are our consolation. I've had great prunes from California and huge fantastic prunes from Agen in France—I've never met one I didn't like.

You'll notice a very small amount of chocolate in the ingredient list. It's not enough to make this even close to a chocolate ice cream, but it adds a richness, a rounded flavor, and interest. You might serve this with a splash of Armagnac.

STEP 1 Stir together the prunes and Armagnac in a small bowl. Let stand at room temperature, tightly covered, for at least 4 hours, or for up to 2 days.

STEP 2 Heat the half-and-half and cream in a medium heavy saucepan over medium heat just until hot.

STEP 3 Whisk together the egg yolks, sugar, and salt in a medium bowl. Slowly pour in the hot half-and-half mixture, whisking constantly. Return to the saucepan and cook, whisking constantly, over medium-low heat until the custard has thickened and coats the back of a spoon; if you draw your finger across it, it should leave a track. Do not let the custard boil or scorch on the bottom; if tiny bubbles appear around the edges, remove the pan from the heat for a few minutes to cool the custard, continuing to whisk. Whisk in the chocolate and vanilla.

STEP 4 Pour the custard through a fine strainer set over a large glass measure or bowl. Let cool to room temperature, whisking occasionally, then refrigerate, tightly covered, for 3 hours, or until thoroughly chilled, or for up to 1 day.

STEP 5 Stir the prunes into the custard. Pour the mixture into an ice-cream maker and freeze according to the manufacturer's instructions. Transfer to a freezer container and freeze for at least 2 hours before serving.

STEP 6 To serve, spoon the ice cream into serving bowls or glasses.

One	8-ounce package pitted prunes, coarsely chopped
3	tablespoons Armagnac or other brandy
2	cups half-and-half
¾	cup heavy (whipping) cream
8	large egg yolks
½	cup plus 2 tablespoons packed dark brown sugar
	Pinch of salt
½	ounce bittersweet or semisweet chocolate, finely chopped
1	teaspoon pure vanilla extract

coconut ice cream with lemongrass and kaffir lime leaves

SERVES 4 TO 6

This recipe begins with a make-your-own coconut milk using toasted coconut, which really adds to the flavor, rather than canned coconut milk. It's lovely served with small scoops of passion fruit or mango sorbet and/or over thin slices of roasted or grilled pineapple. If you were eating this ice cream in Thailand, it would be topped by fresh palm seeds, which, unfortunately, aren't available here. But you could serve it with fresh or drained canned lychees or rambutans on the side, or with thick strips of totally ripe mango. Or simply toast a little extra coconut to use as a garnish. Both lemongrass and lime leaves are available in Thai and many other Asian markets.

1 ½	cups finely grated unsweetened coconut
2	cups heavy (whipping) cream
2	cups half-and-half
4	stalks lemongrass, thinly sliced
8	fresh or thawed frozen kaffir lime leaves, finely shredded
	Pinch of salt
6	large egg yolks
½	cup packed light brown sugar

STEP 1 Preheat the oven to 325°F.

STEP 2 Spread the coconut on a large baking sheet and toast for 6 to 8 minutes, stirring every 2 minutes, until light golden brown; watch it carefully, as it will brown quickly.

STEP 3 Transfer the coconut to a large heavy saucepan. Add the cream, half-and-half, lemongrass, lime leaves, and salt and bring just to a boil over medium-high heat. Remove the pan from the heat and let stand, covered, for 45 minutes.

STEP 4 Pour the cream mixture through a fine strainer set over a large glass measure or a bowl, pressing hard on the solids to extract as much liquid as possible. Set the saucepan aside.

STEP 5 Whisk together the egg yolks and sugar in a medium bowl. Slowly pour in the cream mixture, whisking constantly. Return to the saucepan and cook, whisking constantly, over medium-low heat until the custard has thickened and coats the back of a spoon; if you draw your finger across it, it should leave a track. Do not let the custard boil or scorch on the bottom; if tiny bubbles appear around the edges, remove the pan from the heat for a few minutes to cool the custard, continuing to whisk.

STEP 6 Pour the custard through a fine strainer set over a large glass measure or bowl. Let cool, whisking occasionally, then refrigerate, tightly covered, for at least 3 hours, or until thoroughly chilled, or for up to 1 day.

STEP 7 When ready to freeze, pour the mixture into an ice-cream maker and freeze according to the manufacturer's instructions. Transfer to a freezer container and freeze for at least 2 hours before serving.

STEP 8 To serve, spoon the ice cream into serving bowls or glasses.

lemon meringue ice cream

SERVES 4 TO 6

This ice cream has the perfect balance of sweet and tart, and it's very creamy. The pieces of meringue in the ice cream won't be crunchy, as you might expect, but they are definitely there and have a very nice texture. If you'd like, you can use about three cups of crumbled store-bought meringues, but they may be sweeter than this meringue, so adjust the flavoring accordingly, adding less sugar and/or more lemon juice to the ice cream mixture. You might serve this garnished with a pinch of Lemon Crunch (page 146).

2	large egg whites
	Salt
⅓	cup plus ½ cup sugar
1	cup heavy (whipping) cream
1	cup half-and-half
1	tablespoon finely grated lemon zest
8	large egg yolks
½	cup plus 1 tablespoon fresh lemon juice

LUSCIOUS CREAMY DESSERTS

STEP 1 Position a rack in the middle of the oven and preheat the oven to 250°F. Line the bottom and sides of a 9-inch square baking pan with parchment paper, using tape to secure the paper so it won't slip when you add the meringue.

STEP 2 With an electric mixer on medium speed, beat the egg whites and a pinch of salt in a medium bowl just until foamy. Increase the speed to medium-high and beat just until the whites form soft peaks when the beaters are lifted. Add ⅓ cup of the sugar about 1 tablespoon at a time, then beat just until the whites form stiff peaks. Transfer the meringue to the baking pan and spread evenly with a rubber spatula.

STEP 3 Bake for 1 ½ hours, or until firm to the touch. Transfer the meringue, on the paper, to a wire rack and let cool to room temperature.

STEP 4 Working over a bowl, break the meringue into pieces from ½ to 1 inch in size; the pieces don't have to be exactly this size, and bigger is better than smaller. (The meringue can be made up to 3 days ahead and stored in an airtight container.)

STEP 5 Bring the cream, half-and-half, zest, and a pinch of salt just to a boil in a large heavy saucepan over medium heat, stirring constantly. Remove the pan from the heat and let stand, covered, for 10 minutes.

STEP 6 Whisk together the egg yolks and the remaining ½ cup sugar in a medium bowl. Slowly pour in the cream mixture, whisking constantly. Return to the saucepan and cook, whisking constantly, over medium-low heat until the custard has thickened and coats the back of a spoon; if you draw your finger across it, it should leave a track. Do not let the custard boil or scorch on the bottom; if tiny bubbles appear around the edges, remove the pan from the heat for a few minutes to cool the custard, continuing to whisk.

STEP 7 Pour the custard through a fine strainer set over a large glass measure or bowl. Whisk in the lemon juice. Let cool, whisking occasionally, then refrigerate, tightly covered, for at least 3 hours, until thoroughly chilled, or for up to 1 day.

STEP 8 When ready to freeze, pour the custard mixture into an ice-cream maker and freeze according to the man-ufacturer's instructions. Transfer to a freezer container and gently stir in the meringue. Freeze for at least 2 hours before serving.

STEP 9 To serve, spoon the ice cream into serving bowls or glasses.

caramelized honey ice cream with rosemary and orange

SERVES 6 TO 8

Have you ever had caramelized honey? It's delicious and much easier and quicker to make than caramelizing sugar, and it might change your life—you may start using it with all kinds of things. If you have trouble transferring the honey from the saucepan to the cream mixture, just add a little of the cream mixture to it to soften it up. This is delightful served with candied orange peel and Honey Caramel Sauce (page 137).

½	cup honey
2	cups heavy (whipping) cream
1 ½	cups whole milk
Two	6-inch sprigs fresh rosemary
5	strips orange zest, removed with a vegetable peeler
8	large egg yolks
½	cup sugar
	Pinch of salt
½	cup fresh orange juice
	Honey Caramel Sauce (page 137; optional)

STEP 1 Bring the honey to a boil in a medium heavy saucepan over medium heat. Boil for 5 minutes, or until darkened, but not burned, and very fragrant. Remove the pan from the heat.

STEP 2 Bring the cream and milk just to a boil in a large heavy saucepan over medium heat. Stir in the rosemary and zest, remove the pan from the heat, and let stand, covered, for 15 minutes.

STEP 3 Discard the rosemary and zest. Whisk the honey into the cream mixture and cook, whisking occasionally, over low heat for a few minutes, until well combined and smooth.

STEP 4 Whisk together the egg yolks, sugar, and salt in a medium bowl. Slowly pour in the warm cream mixture, whisking constantly. Return to the saucepan and cook, whisking constantly, over medium-low heat until the custard has thickened and coats the back of a spoon; if you draw your finger across it, it should leave a track. Do not let the custard boil or scorch on the bottom; if tiny bubbles appear around the edges, remove the pan from the heat for a few minutes to cool the custard, continuing to whisk.

STEP 5 Pour the custard through a fine strainer set over a large glass measure or bowl. Whisk in the orange juice. Let cool to room temperature, whisking occasionally, then refrigerate, tightly covered, for 3 hours, or until thoroughly chilled, or for up to 1 day.

STEP 6 When ready to freeze, pour the mixture into an ice-cream maker and freeze according to the manufacturer's instructions. Transfer to a freezer container and freeze for at least 2 hours before serving.

STEP 7 To serve, spoon the ice cream into serving bowls or glasses. Drizzle with the honey caramel sauce, if desired.

espresso granita con panna

SERVES 4

Espresso granita is one of the world's best "cream vehicles." Using an espresso maker for the coffee will give you about one-quarter cup good strong espresso per batch, so you will need to make many cups. If you'd rather, use a French press and make all the coffee at once. (Please feel free to use decaffeinated coffee.) When you pull your spoon from the bottom to the top of your cup, you will get three great textures: cream, icy shards of granita, and the frozen combination of the two. It's bliss.

2	cups hot espresso or very strong coffee
½	cup packed light brown sugar
	Pinch of salt
½	cup heavy (whipping) cream

STEP 1 Whisk together the espresso, sugar, and salt in a medium bowl until the sugar is dissolved. Cool to room temperature, then refrigerate, tightly covered, for 1 hour, or until thoroughly chilled.

STEP 2 Pour the mixture into an 8-inch square baking pan. Cover tightly with foil and freeze for 1 hour, or until frozen around the edges. With a fork, scrape the ice at the edges into the center. Repeat the process every 30 minutes for 2 hours, or until semifirm.

STEP 3 When ready to serve, with an electric mixer on medium-high speed, beat the cream in a medium bowl just until stiff peaks form when the beaters are lifted.

STEP 4 Spoon ¼ cup of the whipped cream into each of four glass cups or short glasses. Scrape across the surface of the granita with a fork, transferring the ice shards to the cups. Serve immediately.

mango kulfi

SERVES 8

Kulfi, the classic Indian ice cream, is sold as a Popsicle on the streets in my neighborhood and all over South Asia. Mango is the most popular flavor, but rose and pistachio are close behind. You can put a Popsicle stick in each cup of kulfi before freezing if you like. I use Ratnā or Swad brand sweetened mango pulp from India. It's the same incredibly sweet, luscious mango used to make mango lassis in Indian restaurants. You could serve this with diced fresh mango and sliced ripe strawberries tossed with lime juice.

3	cups heavy (whipping) cream
1	cup whole milk
1	cup canned sweetened mango pulp
¼	cup packed light brown sugar
	Pinch of salt

STEP 1 Bring the cream and milk to a boil in a large heavy saucepan over high heat, stirring occasionally. Reduce the heat to low and cook at a bare simmer, stirring frequently, for about 1 ½ hours, until the mixture is reduced by about one-third and is thickened.

STEP 2 Whisk the mango, sugar, and salt into the cream mixture. Bring to a simmer over medium-low heat, stirring frequently until the sugar is dissolved; do not boil. Pour through a fine strainer set over a large glass measure or bowl. Let cool to room temperature.

STEP 3 Divide the kulfi among eight 4-ounce paper cups or similar molds. Cover tightly with foil and freeze for at least 8 hours, until firm, or for up to 2 days.

STEP 4 To serve, remove the paper cups and place the kulfi on small plates, with the narrow end up.

creamy special favorites

Here's a collection of creamy desserts from around the world. There are a few from France, a traditional dessert from Venice, a flan inspired by Spain, an all-American shortcake, and a Thai-inspired treat. The Thai-Style Sticky Rice with Coconut Milk and Mangoes (page 126) is a rice pudding prepared with fragrant sticky rice, coconut milk, sugar, and salt. It may not replace your Mom's rice pudding in your heart, but you'll love it—especially if you use absolutely ripe mangoes. Oeufs à la Neige (page 121), which translates as "snow eggs," is a dessert of celestial puffy meringues that look like large eggs, floating in a snowy custard sauce. With the addition of a swirl of strawberry sauce and caramel-coated strawberries, it is better than ever. Paris-Brest with Hazelnut Praline Cream (page 115), another French classic, is made with *pâte à choux*, the pastry of éclairs, and a luscious hazelnut praline pastry cream folded into whipped cream. It's delicious and extravagantly gorgeous. The quenelles of the Chocolate Quenelles with Custard Sauce and Praline (page 129) are small egg-shaped confections, also floating in custard sauce, served topped with crunchy praline—and really, really good. Who doesn't love a flan? The Café con Leche Flan (page 127) is coffee-flavored and lighter than air. The Creamy Caramel Apple Shortcakes (page 117) are perfect for fall and winter, with all the great flavor of rich, sweet, caramelized apple slices. The biscuits, which we Americans do so well, are made with whipped cream and almost float off your plate. And do try the Venetian-Style Fried Custard (page 123). All you do is make a very thick custard and chill it, then cut it into squares, coat it with confectioners' sugar, egg, and fine dry bread crumbs tossed with finely grated lemon zest, and fry it. It is bliss.

paris-brest with hazelnut praline cream

SERVES 8 TO 10

This is a truly grand presentation. When you really need an elaborate and decorative dessert, serve a Paris-Brest. It makes a perfect holiday dessert. It was named for a bike race from Paris to Brittany, in Breton, and back again—thus, a round pastry for a round-trip. Or is it round for the bicycle wheel? You decide. Don't put the dessert together until you're ready to serve it. For this version, you don't even need a pastry bag.

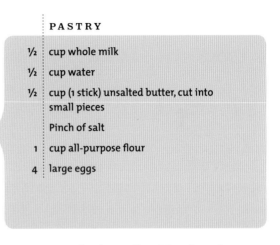

PASTRY

½	cup whole milk
½	cup water
½	cup (1 stick) unsalted butter, cut into small pieces
	Pinch of salt
1	cup all-purpose flour
4	large eggs

PASTRY CREAM

2	cups whole milk
3	large egg yolks
⅓	cup sugar
3	tablespoons cornstarch
	Pinch of salt
1	teaspoon pure vanilla extract

STEP 1 To make the pastry cream: Heat the milk in a medium saucepan over medium-high heat just until hot. Whisk together the egg yolks, sugar, cornstarch, and salt in a medium bowl until blended. Slowly pour in the warm milk, whisking constantly. Return the mixture to the saucepan and cook over medium-low heat, whisking constantly, until the mixture thickens and begins to bubble around the edges. Simmer, whisking, for 1 minute.

STEP 2 Immediately pour the mixture through a coarse strainer set over a medium glass measure or bowl. Whisk in the vanilla. Cover the surface directly with plastic wrap to prevent a skin from forming and let cool to room temperature, then refrigerate for at least 2 hours, until thoroughly chilled, or for up to 1 day.

STEP 3 Position a rack in the middle of the oven and preheat the oven to 425°F. Butter and flour a large baking sheet. Using a 9-inch cake pan as a guide, trace a circle on the baking sheet. With kitchen shears, cut a 1-inch opening from a bottom corner of a large self-sealing plastic bag; set aside.

STEP 4 To make the pastry: Bring the milk, water, butter, and salt to a boil in a large heavy saucepan over high heat. Remove the pan from the heat, add the flour all at once, and stir vigorously with a wooden spoon until the mixture pulls away from the sides of the pan, forming a ball. Transfer the mixture to a large deep bowl and beat with an electric mixer on high speed for 1 minute to cool slightly. *continued ...*

paris-brest with hazelnut praline cream
... continued

Beat in the eggs one at a time, beating well after each addition and scraping down the sides of the bowl as necessary. Beat on medium-high speed for 5 to 7 minutes, until the dough is smooth and dry-looking and has cooled to room temperature.

STEP 5 Spoon the dough into the plastic bag and squeeze it down to the corner with the opening. Using the tracing on the baking sheet as guide, pipe a 1-inch-thick ring of dough just inside the circle. Pipe another 1-inch-thick ring outside the first ring, making sure they are touching. Pipe a final ring on top, along the center seam between the first 2 rings, with the remaining dough. With moistened fingers, gently smooth the dough rings.

STEP 6 Bake the ring for 20 minutes. Reduce the oven temperature to 375°F and bake for 25 more minutes, or until golden brown, puffed, and crisp.

STEP 7 Remove the ring from the oven and poke the sides in 12 places with a toothpick, then bake for 15 more minutes longer. Transfer the ring to a wire rack to cool completely.

STEP 8 To make the hazelnut praline cream: Break the praline into small pieces. Transfer to a heavy-duty self-sealing plastic bag and seal the bag, pressing out the excess air. Coarsely crush the praline with a rolling pin or the bottom of a heavy skillet. Transfer 1 cup of the praline to a food processor and pulse until finely ground.

STEP 9 With a long serrated knife, slice the ring horizontally in half. Carefully discard any wet uncooked dough in the center. With an electric mixer on medium-high speed, beat the cream and the 1 tablespoon confectioners' sugar in a medium bowl until the cream forms stiff peaks when the beaters are lifted. With the same beaters, in another medium bowl, beat the pastry cream on medium speed until smooth. With a whisk or a rubber spatula, fold the finely ground praline into the pastry cream, then fold in the whipped cream. Spoon the cream into the bottom of the ring. Replace the top of the ring.

STEP 10 Dust the ring with confectioners' sugar and top with the coarsely ground praline. Serve immediately, cut into slices with the serrated knife.

HAZELNUT PRALINE CREAM

Praline (page 144), made with hazelnuts

1 cup heavy (whipping) cream

1 tablespoon confectioners' sugar, plus additional for dusting

creamy **caramel apple** shortcakes

SERVES 4

Remember those caramel apples on a stick? They weren't as good as this! The shortcakes are even better served with a scoop of vanilla ice cream. Don't make the shortcake biscuits more than an hour or so ahead of serving them.

SHORTCAKES

1 ¾	cups all-purpose flour
3	tablespoons sugar, plus additional for sprinkling
1	tablespoon baking powder
	Pinch of salt
1 ½	teaspoons finely grated lemon zest
1	cup heavy (whipping) cream
1	teaspoon pure vanilla extract
	Milk for brushing

STEP 1 To make the shortcakes: Position a rack in the middle of the oven and preheat the oven to 425°F. Butter a baking sheet.

STEP 2 Sift together the flour, sugar, baking powder, and salt into a medium bowl. Whisk in the zest.

STEP 3 With an electric mixer on medium-high speed, beat the cream and vanilla in a medium deep bowl just until the cream holds soft peaks when the beaters are lifted. Make a well in the center of the dry ingredients, add the cream, and stir with a fork just until it begins to form a dough; it will be very sticky.

STEP 4 On a lightly floured surface, knead the dough about 6 times, just until it is well combined. Roll or pat it out to ¾ inch thick. With a floured 3 ½-inch cutter, cut out 4 rounds, gathering and rerolling the scraps as necessary. Transfer the rounds to the baking sheet. Brush with milk and sprinkle with sugar. *continued ...*

creamy caramel apple shortcakes

... continued

CARAMEL APPLES

4	medium tart cooking apples, such as Granny Smith (about 1 ½ pounds)
2	tablespoons unsalted butter
½	cup Caramel Sauce (page 135)
	Vanilla ice cream for serving (optional)

STEP 5 Bake for 15 to 17 minutes, until golden brown. Transfer with a wide metal spatula to a wire rack to cool.

STEP 6 Meanwhile, make the caramel apples: Peel and core the apples and cut each one into 8 wedges. Melt the butter in a large heavy skillet over medium-high heat. Add the apples and cook, stirring occasionally, for about 10 minutes, until lightly browned. Stir in the caramel sauce and boil, stirring gently, for 4 minutes, or until the apples are soft. Remove from the heat.

STEP 7 Split each shortcake in half. Arrange the bottom halves on dessert plates, spoon the apples over them, and add the tops. Drizzle with any remaining sauce and serve immediately, with ice cream, if using.

oeufs à la **neige** with **custard** and **strawberry sauce**

SERVES 6

There are very good reasons this classic has been so well loved for so many years. The wispy, cloudlike meringues have a wonderful texture, and they are a perfect contrast with the smooth custard sauce. This version has fresh ripe strawberries as well, and the sprinkle of praline (or Lemon Crunch) on top brings out the best in everything. You could use a mango- or orange-flower-water–flavored custard sauce, if you'd like. You can make the custard the day ahead, but serve the meringues not too long after you make them, and certainly on the same day.

3	large egg whites
1/8	teaspoon cream of tartar
1/3	cup sugar
1/2	teaspoon pure vanilla extract
3	cups whole milk
1 1/2	cups chilled Custard Sauce (page 132)
	Chilled Strawberry Sauce (page 122)
6	Caramel-Coated Strawberries (page 148) or 6 ripe strawberries on the stem for garnish (optional)
	Coarsely or finely ground Praline (page 144) or Lemon Crunch (page 146) for garnish

STEP 1 With an electric mixer on medium speed, beat the egg whites and cream of tartar in a medium bowl just until the egg whites form soft peaks when the beaters are lifted. Increase the speed to medium-high and add the sugar about 1 tablespoon at a time, beating well after each addition, then beat until the whites form stiff peaks. Beat in the vanilla.

STEP 2 Heat the milk in a medium skillet over medium heat just until tiny bubbles form around the edges; do not boil. Reduce the heat to low. Generously fill a 1/2-cup metal measuring cup with meringue. With 2 large spoons, shape it into an oval or egg shape about 3 inches long and gently drop it into the simmering milk mixture. Repeat to make 2 more ovals. (Do not shape more than 3 ovals at a time—the meringues should not touch each other as they poach.) *continued ...*

oeufs à la neige with custard and strawberry sauce ... *continued*

Poach for 4 to 5 minutes, turning once, until the meringues are firm to the touch. Remove the meringues with a slotted spoon and drain on paper towels. Repeat with the remaining meringue mixture, making 6 meringues. Transfer the meringues to a large plate and refrigerate until cold, or for up to 3 hours.

STEP 3 To serve, spoon ¼ cup of the custard sauce onto each dessert plate and drizzle with a generous tablespoon of strawberry sauce. (Reserve the remaining sauce for another dessert.) Gently arrange the meringues on top. Garnish each serving with a strawberry (if using), sprinkle with the praline, and serve immediately.

STRAWBERRY SAUCE (MAKES 1 CUP)

1	pint ripe strawberries, hulled and sliced
2	tablespoons light corn syrup
2	tablespoons water
	Pinch of salt
1	teaspoon fresh lemon juice

STEP 1 Combine the strawberries, corn syrup, water, and salt in a medium saucepan and cook, stirring occasionally, over medium heat for 10 minutes, or until the berries have softened and formed a sauce. Stir in the lemon juice.

STEP 2 Pour the sauce through a fine strainer set over a small bowl, pressing hard on the solids to extract as much liquid as possible. Cool to room temperature, then transfer to a glass jar and refrigerate, tightly covered, until ready to serve. (The sauce can be refrigerated for up to 1 week.) Serve chilled or at room temperature.

venetian-style **fried custard**

SERVES 6 TO 8

The creamy inside and crispy outside of this unusual dessert is a delightful combination. Use a skimmer to keep the oil clean, a probe thermometer to keep track of the oil temperature, and a Microplane to grate the zest.

CUSTARD

6	large egg yolks
1¼	cups sugar
1	cup bread flour
	Pinch of salt
4	cups whole milk
5	strips lemon zest, removed with a vegetable peeler
½	teaspoon pure vanilla extract
	Vegetable oil for deep-frying
	Lemon wedges for serving

STEP 1 To make the custard: Whisk together the egg yolks and sugar in a large heavy saucepan, not over the heat. With a wooden spoon, stir in the flour and salt until well combined. Add 1 cup of the milk and whisk until smooth. Slowly pour in the remaining milk, whisking until smooth. Add the lemon zest and cook over medium heat, whisking frequently at first and constantly toward the end, for 18 to 22 minutes, until the mixute comes to a boil, large bubbles rise to the top, and the custard is very thick. Whisk in the vanilla. Pour the custard through a coarse strainer set over a large glass measure or bowl.

STEP 2 Butter a 9-inch square baking pan. Transfer the custard to the baking pan, place a piece of plastic wrap directly on the custard to keep a skin from forming, and let cool to room temperature on a wire rack. Refrigerate for at least 4 hours, until very firm, or for up to overnight.

STEP 3 Preheat the oven to 250°F. Line a large baking sheet with double layers of paper towels.

STEP 4 Pour about 4 inches of vegetable oil into a Dutch oven and heat the oil to 350°F. Cut the custard into 2-inch squares.

continued ...

venetian-style fried custard ... *continued*

STEP 5 Meanwhile, make the crumb coating: Put the sugar on a medium plate. Lightly beat the eggs in a shallow bowl. Toss the bread crumbs with the zest on a medium plate. Line a large plate with wax paper. Working with 4 or 5 pieces at a time, dust the custard generously with sugar, dip into the beaten eggs, coat in bread crumbs, patting the crumbs onto the custard to coat well, and transfer to the wax-paper-lined plate. Transfer the plate to the refrigerator and coat the remaining custard, adding the squares to the plate.

STEP 6 Deep-fry the custard in batches, keeping the remaining custard squares in the refrigerator while you fry the first batch. Add to the hot oil and cook, turning once, for 2 to 3 minutes, or until golden brown. Transfer to the paper-towel-lined baking sheet and keep warm in the oven. Repeat with the remaining custard squares.

STEP 7 Serve warm, with lemon wedges.

CRUMB COATING

1 ½	cups confectioners' sugar
4	large eggs
1 ½	cups plain fine dried bread crumbs
¼	cup finely grated lemon zest

thai-style sticky rice with coconut milk and mango

SERVES 4

Thais use perfect mangoes for this dish. Always serve the mangoes at room temperature, and never refrigerate them. The classic garnish is toasted mung beans, but the dessert is wonderful without them. It has great texture and a great flavor balance between sweet and salty. Serve the rice warm—it's both creamier and more comforting, and it shouldn't sit around for long, because it will keep absorbing the coconut milk.

The easiest way to rinse the rice is by transferring it back and forth between a large bowl of water, which you use to swirl it around in, and a large coarse strainer. If you're lucky enough to have some fresh or frozen pandan leaves (also known as screw pine leaves, available in many Asian markets), add 3 or 4 to the water before you bring it to a boil.

1 ½	cups Thai sticky rice
2	cups well-stirred canned coconut milk
¼	cup packed light brown sugar or palm sugar
½	teaspoon salt
2	ripe mangoes, peeled, pitted, and thickly sliced

STEP 1 Rinse the rice until the water runs clear. Soak the rice in cool water to cover by at least 2 inches in a medium bowl for at least 3 hours, or for up to 1 day.

STEP 2 Drain the rice in a colander. Wrap it in two layers of rinsed cheesecloth or a kitchen towel and place in a steamer basket over boiling water. Cover and steam for about 30 minutes, or until the rice is tender.

STEP 3 Meanwhile, just before the rice is done, heat the coconut milk, sugar, and salt in a medium saucepan over medium heat until hot, whisking until the sugar is dissolved. Remove from the heat.

STEP 4 Transfer the rice to a medium bowl, add the warm coconut milk mixture, and stir until well combined. (It will look as if there is way too much coconut milk.) Let stand for 10 minutes so the rice can absorb the coconut milk mixture.

STEP 5 Transfer the rice to serving plates, arrange the mango slices on the side, and serve warm.

café con leche flan

SERVES 8

This elegant, silky-smooth custard sports a glistening caramel topping that runs down the sides and pools around the flan when it is unmolded. It is luscious and makes a delightful finish to a meal. You could arrange 2-inch chunks of Praline (page 144) on top of the flan right before serving—use one piece for each serving.

Putting two full pans into the oven is no fun, so I recommend you place the roasting pan for the water bath in the oven, put the cake pan inside it, and then pour the custard into the cake pan and the hot water into the roasting pan. It's easier and safer.

¾	cup sugar
5	tablespoons water
Two	12-ounce cans evaporated milk
One	14-ounce can sweetened condensed milk
2	large eggs
3	large egg whites
1 ½	tablespoons instant espresso powder
1	teaspoon pure vanilla extract
¼	teaspoon salt

STEP 1 Position a rack in the middle of the oven and preheat the oven to 325°F. Have ready a 9-inch round cake pan and a roasting pan. Put on a kettle of water to boil for the water bath.

STEP 2 Bring the sugar and water to a boil in a medium heavy saucepan over medium heat, stirring until the sugar is dissolved. Increase the heat to high and bring the mixture to a boil, washing down the sides of the pan with a wet pastry brush if you see any sugar crystals. Boil, without stirring, swirling the pan toward the end to even out the color, until the caramel is a dark amber color. Immediately pour the caramel into the cake pan, tilting to coat the bottom and sides evenly. Let stand at room temperature until cooled and hardened.

STEP 3 Whisk together the evaporated milk, condensed milk, eggs, egg whites, espresso powder, vanilla, and salt in a large bowl until the espresso powder dissolves and the mixture is smooth. Pour through a fine strainer set over a large glass measure.

STEP 4 Place the roasting pan in the oven, place the cake pan in the roasting pan, and pour the custard into the cake pan. Carefully pour enough boiling water into the roasting pan to reach halfway up the sides of the cake pan. Bake for 1 ¼ to 1 ½ hours, until the edges are set but the center is still slightly jiggly; a small thin knife inserted into the center of the custard should come out clean.

STEP 5 Carefully remove the cake pan from the hot water and transfer to a wire rack to cool completely. Refrigerate, tightly covered, for 3 hours, until thoroughly chilled and set, or for up to 1 day.

STEP 6 To serve, run a thin knife around the edge of the flan and invert it onto a large plate deep enough to hold the runny caramel. Cut into wedges, spooning on any extra caramel.

chocolate quenelles with custard sauce and praline

SERVES 8

This is fantastic served with fresh fruit. Try ripe raspberries, blackberries, sliced juicy plums, or clementine wedges. If you don't want to use the Praline for garnish, try Crunchy Nuts (page 145) made with pistachios, Lemon Crunch (page 146), or a tiny drizzle of Caramel Sauce (page 135).

1	cup heavy (whipping) cream
½	cup whole milk
8	ounces bittersweet or semisweet chocolate, finely chopped
4	large egg yolks
¼	cup packed light brown sugar
2	cups chilled Custard Sauce (page 132)
2	tablespoons finely ground Praline (page 144) for garnish

STEP 1 Bring the cream and milk just to a boil in a medium saucepan over medium heat. Remove the pan from the heat and whisk in the chocolate. Let stand for 2 minutes, then whisk until smooth.

STEP 2 With an electric mixer on medium-high speed, beat the egg yolks and sugar in a medium deep bowl for about 4 minutes, until thick and pale. Reduce the speed to low and slowly beat in the chocolate mixture. Pour through a fine strainer set over a freezer container with a tight-fitting lid. Pack down to force out air bubbles. Freeze, tightly covered, for at least 3 hours, until firm, or for up to 3 days.

STEP 3 Shape the chocolate mixture into 24 quenelles, or ovals, using 2 large tablespoons of the same size. Hold a spoon in each hand, with the bowls facing each other. With one spoon, scoop up a heaping spoonful of the chocolate mixture. Press the second spoon against the side of the chocolate mixture and scoop it out of the first spoon—you should have an oval with a nice smooth side from the first spoon. Repeat, scraping the quenelle from the second spoon back into the first spoon, to finish shaping it. If it's not shaped to your liking, keep scooping until you have a nice three-sided football shape. (Or use an oval scoop.) Transfer the quenelles to a small baking sheet lined with wax paper and continue making quenelles. Refrigerate until serving time.

STEP 4 To serve, spoon about ¼ cup of the custard sauce onto each serving plate. Place 3 quenelles in the middle of each pool of custard and sprinkle with the praline.

sauces and a syrup

Keep custard and caramel sauces in the refrigerator, and praline powder in your freezer, and you will be prepared for anything. The Luscious Creamy Custard Sauce (page 132) is exceptionally versatile. You can use it with just about any dessert or as a component of other sauces, such as Custard & Cream & Caramel Sauce (page 134) or Sauce à la Ritz (page 134). All of these will turn ripe summer fruits or berries or winter fruit compotes into a divine dessert—just like that.

Don't be intimidated by the idea of caramel. There are huge rewards from having a jar of caramel sauce in your refrigerator. Start with the Honey Caramel Sauce (page 137), which is foolproof and very quickly made. In just five minutes or so, you caramelize the honey, which really enhances its flavor. Another wildly luxurious sauce is the Caramel Mascarpone Cream (page 136). Just heavy cream, mascarpone, and caramel sauce whipped together, it has the most amazing texture. Newfangled Caramel Sauce (page 135) is the epitome of scrumptious, made with caramelized sugar, heavy cream, crème fraîche, and just a bit of fresh lemon juice to balance the flavors. Almost anything would taste better with a drizzle or a pool. There's also a Caramel Syrup (page 138) included here, to use as a drizzle or a drop garnish to add another dimension to whatever dessert you are serving. It's a component of the caramel oranges for the Coeur à la Crème (page 86).

Of course you'll find a Chocolate Sauce (page 140) here. Made with dark chocolate, milk or water, and cream, it is swanky, simple, and sublime. Or make one of the many variations— my favorite is the Chocolate Praline Sauce (page 140). And there's a true Butterscotch Sauce (page 139), real butterscotch made with butter, dark brown sugar, cream, and just a smidgen of molasses, which has a wonderful deep flavor. You'll find many uses for it.

luscious creamy **custard sauce**

MAKES A SCANT 3 CUPS

Also known as English cream or crème anglaise, this sauce has scores of uses. It also has almost infinite possibilities for variation. I prefer it made with half-and-half, but you can use heavy cream, all milk, or milk and half-and-half, depending on your mood. You might use less sugar and whisk in some Caramel Sauce (page 135) or Praline (page 144) after straining it. Or steep strips of citrus zest or grated zest—Meyer lemon, tangerine, clementine, mandarin, or lime—in the half-and-half and add fresh citrus juice to taste after making the sauce. Herbs are a great addition also; try steeping basil, tarragon, rosemary, lemon verbena, scented geranium leaves, or lemon thyme in the half-and-half.

2	cups half-and-half
6	large egg yolks
½	cup sugar
	Pinch of salt
1	teaspoon pure vanilla paste or extract

STEP 1 Heat the half-and-half in a medium heavy saucepan over medium heat just until hot. Remove the pan from the heat.

STEP 2 Whisk together the egg yolks, sugar, and salt in a medium bowl. Slowly pour in the hot half-and-half, whisking constantly. Return to the saucepan and cook, whisking constantly, over medium-low heat until the custard has thickened and coats the back of a spoon; if you draw your finger across it, it should leave a track. Do not let the sauce boil or scorch on the bottom; if tiny bubbles appear around the edges, remove the pan from the heat for a few minutes to cool the custard, continuing to whisk.

STEP 3 Pour the custard through a fine strainer set over a medium glass measure or bowl. Let cool to room temperature, whisking occasionally to keep a skin from forming, then whisk in the vanilla. Serve, or refrigerate, tightly covered, for about 3 hours, or for up to 4 days. Serve chilled, or reheat gently to serve warm.

variations

Pumpkin Custard Sauce

Make the sauce with 1 ½ cups half-and-half. Add
¾ cup canned pumpkin purée (not pumpkin pie mix)
and ⅛ teaspoon pumpkin pie spice to the egg yolks.

Sesame Custard Sauce

Add 1 teaspoon Asian (toasted) sesame oil instead of
the vanilla. Serve with sliced ripe fruit.

Orange Flower Water or Rose Water Custard Sauce

Stir in about a teaspoon of either instead of the vanilla.

Mango Custard Sauce

Add ¾ cup canned sweetened mango purée and a
squeeze of fresh lime juice to the finished sauce.

Spiked Custard Sauce

Add 2 to 4 tablespoons of your favorite liqueur, spirit,
or eau-de-vie.

sauce à la ritz

MAKES ABOUT 2 CUPS

I can't think of anything this wouldn't be good with, though I do think it is just perfect with fruit and berries of all kinds. I'm sure you will like it too. I found the idea in Louis Diat's terrific book, *Sauces*, but I drastically changed the proportions. The original had enough Grand Marnier in it to be a drink!

1	cup heavy (whipping) cream
½	cup chilled Custard Sauce (page 132)
2	tablespoons Grand Marnier or other liqueur

With an electric mixer on medium-high speed, beat the cream in a large deep bowl just until stiff peaks form when the beaters are lifted. Whisk together the custard sauce and Grand Marnier in a small bowl, add to the cream, and beat just until stiff peaks form again. Use immediately.

custard & cream & caramel sauce

MAKES ABOUT 1½ CUPS

One of my favorite things to serve this with is baked apples or other roasted fruit.

¼	cup chilled Custard Sauce (page 132)
2	tablespoons chilled Caramel Sauce (page 135)
½	cup heavy (whipping) cream

STEP 1 Whisk together the custard and caramel sauces in a small bowl.

STEP 2 With an electric mixer on medium-high speed, beat the cream in a medium deep bowl just until stiff peaks form when the beaters are lifted. Add the custard mixture and beat just until stiff peaks form again. Use immediately, or refrigerate, tightly covered, for up to 2 hours.

variation

Custard & Cream & Praline Sauce
Omit the caramel sauce. Beat the cream with a pinch of salt just until the cream forms stiff peaks. Add the custard sauce and beat just until stiff peaks form again. Whisk in 3 tablespoons finely ground Praline (page 144).

newfangled caramel sauce

MAKES 3 CUPS

I say make enough of this to have it around! You'll find millions of uses for it. I call it new-fangled because it has crème fraîche and fresh lemon juice in it, which balance the caramel flavor perfectly.

1	cup heavy (whipping) cream
½	cup crème fraîche, homemade (page 12) or store-bought, or additional heavy (whipping) cream
2	cups sugar
½	cup water
2	tablespoons light corn syrup
	Pinch of salt
2	teaspoons fresh lemon juice

STEP 1 Combine the heavy cream and crème fraîche in a small saucepan and cook over medium heat, whisking occasionally, until hot. Set aside, covered, to keep warm.

STEP 2 Heat the sugar, water, corn syrup, and salt in a large heavy saucepan over medium heat, stirring, until the sugar is dissolved. Increase the heat to high and bring the mixture to a boil, washing down the sides of the pan with a wet pastry brush if you see any sugar crystals. Boil, without stirring, swirling the pan toward the end to even out the color, until the caramel is a dark amber color. Immediately remove the saucepan from the heat. Let stand for about 1 minute, or until most of the bubbles have subsided.

STEP 3 Being careful to avoid the spatters, stir in the cream mixture about 2 tablespoons at a time. Return the pan to low heat and cook, whisking, until the sauce is smooth. Remove the pan from the heat and stir in the lemon juice. Use immediately, or let cool to room temperature and refrigerate, tightly covered, for up to 2 months. Gently reheat the sauce before serving, if desired, adding a little water or cream if necessary to thin it slightly.

variations

Banana Caramel Sauce
Add 1 or 2 mashed ripe bananas along with the cream mixture.

Chocolate Caramel Sauce
Whisk in 6 ounces bittersweet or semisweet chocolate, melted, along with 3 tablespoons warm water after stirring in the cream mixture.

Buttery Caramel Sauce
Stir in 2 or 3 tablespoons unsalted butter, cut into small pieces, after adding the cream.

Ginger Caramel Sauce
Add ¼ cup minced crystallized ginger to the cream before heating it and let steep while you make the caramel. Strain the cream or not before adding it to the caramel, depending on your preference.

Saffron Caramel Sauce
Add a couple of large pinches of crumbled saffron threads to the cream before heating it and let steep while you make the caramel. Strain the cream before adding it to the caramel. Also try cardamom seeds, a cinnamon stick or two, whole cloves, or allspice.

caramel mascarpone cream

MAKES ABOUT 1½ CUPS

Like almost anything prepared with mascarpone, this sauce has a wonderful texture. It's brilliant served with the Brown Butter–Crème Fraîche Pound Cake (page 43), the Pumpkin Cheesecake (page 53), the Lemon and Ginger Brioche Bread Pudding (page 87), or the Creamy Caramel Apple Shortcakes (page 117). It's quite nice served dusted with coarsely or finely ground Praline (page 144).

1 cup mascarpone cheese

½ cup heavy (whipping) cream

¾ cup chilled Caramel Sauce (page 135)

With an electric mixer on medium-high speed, beat together the mascarpone and cream in a medium deep bowl just until the mixture forms stiff peaks when the beaters are lifted. Add the caramel sauce and beat until well combined. Use immediately, or refrigerate, tightly covered, for up to 2 days.

caramel **whipped** cream

MAKES A SCANT 2 CUPS

This is the little black dress of sauces.

½	cup heavy (whipping) cream
¼	cup crème fraîche, homemade (page 12) or store-bought, or additional heavy (whipping) cream
½	cup chilled Caramel Sauce (page 135)

With an electric mixer on medium-high speed, beat the heavy cream and crème fraîche in a medium deep bowl just until stiff peaks form when the beaters are lifted. With a whisk or a rubber spatula, fold in the caramel sauce. Serve immediately, or refrigerate, tightly covered, for up to 4 hours.

honey caramel sauce

MAKES ABOUT 2 CUPS

A caramel sauce for honey lovers. While not technically caramel, it's quicker to make than ordinary caramel sauce and it won't crystallize.

1 ½	cups honey
½	cup heavy (whipping) cream
	Pinch of salt
2	teaspoons fresh lemon juice
½	teaspoon pure vanilla extract

STEP 1 Bring the honey to a boil in a medium heavy saucepan over medium-high heat. Boil for 5 minutes, or until darkened, but not burned, and very fragrant. Reduce the heat to medium-low and slowly and carefully pour in the cream. Add the salt, bring to a boil over medium heat, and boil for 5 minutes, or until slightly thickened; the sauce will thicken further as it stands.

STEP 2 Add the lemon juice and vanilla and pour the sauce through a fine strainer set over a medium glass measure or bowl. Serve hot or warm, or let cool and refrigerate, tightly covered, for up to 2 months. Serve chilled, or gently reheat the sauce before serving, adding a little water or cream if necessary to thin it slightly.

caramel syrup

MAKES 3 CUPS

This is one of my most important dessert staples. It has an almost unlimited number of uses, and putting it to use takes no time at all. Rather than adding a single note of sweetness to a dessert, as sugar does, caramel syrup adds bittersweet, which is more complex, delicious, and interesting. Think of it—you'd never dip a spoon into the sugar bowl for a treat, but who can resist a spoonful of caramel syrup? Fold some of the syrup into a bowl of fresh fruit; drizzle it over cakes, pies, meringue, and ice cream desserts; or add it to drinks. What ideas do you have? This is a big batch, but it keeps well for a good long time.

3	cups sugar
2	cups warm water
¼	cup light corn syrup
¼	teaspoon salt

STEP 1 Heat the sugar, 1 cup of the water, the corn syrup, and salt in a large heavy saucepan over medium heat, stirring, until the sugar is dissolved. Increase the heat to high and bring the mixture to a boil, washing down the sides of the pan with a wet pastry brush if you see any sugar crystals. Boil, without stirring, swirling the pan toward the end to even out the color, until the caramel is a dark amber color.

STEP 2 Immediately remove the saucepan from the heat and, being careful to avoid the spatters, add the remaining 1 cup warm water about 2 tablespoons at a time. Return the pan to low heat and cook, whisking, until the syrup is smooth. Use immediately, or let cool and refrigerate, tightly covered, for up to 3 months. Serve chilled or at room temperature, or gently reheat before serving.

butterscotch sauce

MAKES ABOUT 2½ CUPS

Quite different from caramel sauce but just as good, this is made with molasses, dark brown sugar, and butter. Butterscotch may be one of the best fragrances in your kitchen as well as a fantastic flavor. It also takes less time to make than caramel sauce. Serve this over ice cream, fruit, or whatever appeals to you. You could replace a tablespoon or so of the dark brown sugar with dark muscovado sugar.

6	tablespoons (¾ stick) unsalted butter
¾	cup packed dark brown sugar
2	teaspoons dark molasses
	Pinch of salt
1½	cups heavy (whipping) cream

Melt the butter in a large heavy saucepan over medium heat. Add the sugar, molasses, and salt and cook, whisking, until the mixture is liquid; the sugar will not dissolve completely. Increase the heat to medium-high, slowly pour in the cream, and bring to a boil. Boil for 3 minutes. Serve warm, or let cool and refrigerate, tightly covered, for up to 3 weeks. Reheat gently before serving.

chocolate sauce

MAKES ABOUT 2 CUPS

You can use either milk or water for this sauce. You might not think water would make a good chocolate sauce, but, in fact, it gives the chocolate sauce a stronger chocolate flavor. Notice there is no added sugar—that too makes for more chocolate flavor.

8	ounces bittersweet or semisweet chocolate, finely chopped
1	cup whole milk or water
½	cup crème fraîche, homemade (page 12) or store-bought, or heavy (whipping) cream
	Pinch of salt

Place the chocolate in a medium heatproof bowl. Bring the milk, crème fraîche, and salt just to a boil, whisking occasionally, in a small saucepan over medium heat. Pour the mixture over the chocolate and let stand for 2 minutes, then whisk until smooth. Serve hot or warm, or cool to room temperature and refrigerate, tightly covered, for about 2 hours, until thoroughly chilled, or for up to 2 weeks. If serving chilled, whisk the sauce before serving. Reheat gently to serve warm.

variations

Chocolate Praline Sauce
Stir ½ cup coarsely ground Praline (page 144) into the sauce. Serve warm.

Chocolate Sauce with Brandy, Rum, or Liqueur
Stir in 1 to 2 tablespoons of brandy, rum, or your favorite liqueur.

meringue cream

MAKES A SCANT 3 CUPS

The combination of whipped egg whites and cream give this sauce a fine light foamy texture, like a mousse. It is wonderful alongside many, many desserts. Try it on the side with fancy cakes and tarts, simple fruit desserts, and everything in between.

2	large egg whites
6	tablespoons sugar
¾	cup heavy (whipping) cream
¾	teaspoon pure vanilla paste or extract

STEP 1 At least 30 minutes before serving, with an electric mixer on medium-high speed, beat the egg whites in a medium deep bowl just until the whites form soft peaks when the beaters are lifted. Gradually beat in the sugar, about 1 tablespoon at a time, and continue to beat until the whites form stiff peaks.

STEP 2 In another medium deep bowl, with the mixer on medium-high speed, beat the cream with the vanilla just until the cream forms stiff peaks. With a whisk or a rubber spatula, fold the cream into the meringue until well combined. Refrigerate, tightly covered, for at least 20 minutes before serving, or for up to 6 hours.

garnishes and candies

There's not a dessert in this book that must have a garnish, but a little something served on the side is fun and can geometrically increase the pleasure of the dessert. In terms of garnish, creamy desserts call out for a contrast in texture, and that contrast highlights the creaminess. A garnish can be as simple as something that can be picked up in the supermarket: caramel corn, honey-roasted or lightly salted nuts, candied puffed rice, tart apple chips, fruit leather or dried fruit, chopped toffee or buttercrunch, crumbled cookies, even instant espresso powder for sprinkling.

Many of my favorite garnishes for creamy desserts involve caramelized sugar. So here you will find Praline (page 144), the classic French concoction of caramelized sugar and nuts that can be broken into large shards or pieces that look like very shiny glass, or coarsely ground, or ground into a powder. You'll also find Caramel-Coated Strawberries (page 148). Not only are they beautiful—they look as if they are coated with glass—they are a delicious sweet treat. And try the Praline Truffles (page 150); not only are they terrific on the side of a dessert, anyone would love to see one on the side of their cup of coffee or espresso. Your friends and family would also love to find a Luscious Salty Soft Caramel (page 149) placed on the side of a dessert or a cup of coffee. Rich, creamy, and smooth with a great, just slightly salty flavor, they are a delight. The Crunchy Nuts (page 145) are very easy to make, and you end up with terrific caramel-coated individual nuts or clusters of nuts. Lemon Crunch is another terrifically easy garnish, but you'll use it—by the pinch—for garnishing countless desserts. It's nothing more than those chic rough-cut brown sugar cubes and lemon zest stirred together, but it offers a very fresh aroma and a lovely crunch. You'll be amazed at how many ways you find to include it in your dishes. The Lacy Cookie Crisps (page 147) are a terrific garnish for many creamy desserts (they use cookies like these in fancy restaurants all the time). They are a treat with ice creams, puddings, custards, and many other desserts.

praline

MAKES 1 POUND

Whatever nut or combination of nuts you choose to use, give them a nice golden brown color by roasting them first (except for pistachios—they're best not browned). The classic formula for praline is one part nuts to one part sugar, but this recipe is my personal preference, one and a half parts sugar to one part nuts, because I like the caramel intensity. Your choice—use more nuts if you want. After it's made, you can just break up the praline into big pieces, coarsely crush it, or process it to a fine powder, depending on what you're using it for. The powder will spoil quickly at room temperature, so store it in the freezer. You can use any nut you choose—including pine nuts, sesame seeds, and coconut.

1	cup blanched whole almonds
1 ½	cups sugar
⅓	cup water
1	tablespoon light corn syrup
	Pinch of salt

STEP 1 Preheat the oven to 350°F.

STEP 2 Spread the almonds on a baking sheet and toast for about 15 minutes, until golden brown and fragrant. Cool on the pan on a wire rack. When the nuts are cool, push them close together in a single layer.

STEP 3 Heat the sugar, water, corn syrup, and salt in a medium heavy saucepan over medium heat, stirring until the sugar dissolves. Increase the heat to high and bring the mixture to a boil, washing down the sides of the pan with a wet pastry brush if you see any sugar crystals. Boil, without stirring, swirling the pan toward the end to even out the color, until the caramel is a dark amber color. Immediately pour the caramel in a circular motion over the almonds to coat evenly. Let stand for about 15 minutes to cool and harden.

STEP 4 For shards, break into large or medium pieces. For coarsely ground praline, break into smaller pieces, place in a self-sealing plastic bag, and crush with a rolling pin into the size you need. For praline powder, pulse small pieces in a food processor until finely ground.

crunchy nuts

MAKES 2½ CUPS

A sprinkling of these nuts will cut the richness of creamy desserts. Yes, they're rich too, but it works—I think it is simply the contrast of crunchy against creamy. I make these most often with pistachios—they're a great-looking garnish and cooking them with the sugar really enhances their flavor. Toast the nuts first, if you'd like, unless you're using pistachios.

¼	cup sugar
1	tablespoon light corn syrup
1	teaspoon water
	Pinch of salt
1½	cups pistachios or nut of your choice

STEP 1 Preheat the oven to 350°F. Place a silicone baking mat on a large baking sheet.

STEP 2 Heat the sugar, corn syrup, water, and salt in a medium saucepan over low heat, stirring occasionally, until the mixture is liquid; the sugar will not dissolve completely. Remove the pan from the heat and stir in the nuts until well coated. Spread in a thin layer on the silicone mat.

STEP 3 Bake for 5 minutes. Stir gently, and bake for about 15 minutes longer, until golden brown. Let cool on the pan on a wire rack.

STEP 4 Invert the baking mat onto another baking sheet. Break into individual nuts or clusters of nuts. Store at room temperature in an airtight container for up to 1 week.

lemon crunch

Here's an old-fashioned garnish, from the days when there were always sugar cubes around, instead of those little colored packets of all the sweeteners we have now. You can use this as a garnish for many things, but I think it's especially good on the Tarragon Cup Custard (page 71). Not only does it add a very nice crunch, it's very aromatic. You might make this with other zests—tangerine, lime, orange, or clementine.

I have a very heavy large mortar and pestle from Thailand, which makes very short work of the job.

8   rough-cut brown sugar cubes

2   teaspoons finely grated lemon zest

Crush the sugar cubes with a mortar and pestle until broken up into small pieces but still with some texture, not finely ground. Add the zest and stir until well combined. Transfer to a small jar with a tight-fitting lid and store at room temperature for up to 2 weeks.

lacy **cookie crisps**

MAKES ABOUT 30 COOKIES

These special-occasion cookies are very sophisticated and grown-up. If you like, mold each one over a rolling pin immediately after you remove the cookies from the baking sheet to give them a graceful curved shape— what the French call *tuiles*, named after their curved roof tiles. They are a terrific treat with ice creams, puddings, and custards.

½	cup packed light brown sugar
½	cup light corn syrup
6	tablespoons (¾ stick) unsalted butter
1	cup pecans, finely chopped
¾	cup all-purpose flour
½	teaspoon pure vanilla extract

STEP 1 Preheat the oven to 375°F. Butter a large baking sheet.

STEP 2 Bring the brown sugar, corn syrup, and butter to a boil in a medium saucepan over medium heat. Remove the pan from the heat and, with a wooden spoon, stir in the pecans, flour, and vanilla.

STEP 3 Drop 1 level teaspoon of the batter onto the baking sheet. Repeat to make 8 to 10 cookies (depending on size of your baking sheet), placing them at least 3 inches apart. Bake for 5 to 7 minutes, until lightly browned. Remove the baking sheet from the oven, transfer to a wire rack, and let cool for about 1 minute to set slightly.

STEP 4 With a wide metal spatula, quickly loosen the cookies and transfer them to wire racks to cool completely. Repeat with the remaining batter. Store the cookies between layers of wax paper in a large tin or other shallow container for up to 1 day.

caramel-coated strawberries

You may have some caramel left over after dipping the strawberries, but that is better than not having enough. You don't want the caramel to cool down too quickly, or it will be too thick for dipping. So keep the water in the bowl very hot—even if you have to, very quickly, refill it. If your berries don't have stems, and you're not comfortable holding on to the hulls, skewer them with small bamboo skewers to dip, so you don't burn yourself. Use a probe thermometer here if you have one.

1 pint ripe strawberries, preferably with stems

1 cup sugar

3 tablespoons water

2 tablespoons light corn syrup

STEP 1   Butter a baking sheet. Put on a kettle of water to boil. Pat the strawberries dry.

STEP 2   Heat the sugar, water, and corn syrup in a medium heavy saucepan over medium heat, stirring, until the sugar dissolves. Increase the heat to high and bring the mixture to a boil, washing down the sides of the pan with a wet pastry brush if you see any sugar crystals. Boil, without stirring, swirling the pan toward the end to even out the color, until the caramel is a dark amber color and the temperature reaches 300° to 310°F on a probe or candy thermometer. Remove the pan from the heat and immediately set it in a bowl of very hot water to keep it hot.

STEP 3   Working quickly, tilt the saucepan to form a pool of caramel and dip the strawberries, one at a time, into the syrup to coat them completely except for the hulls. Shake off any excess and transfer to the baking sheet. Let cool until set. Serve within an hour, the sooner the better.

luscious **salty soft** caramels

MAKES 64 CARAMELS

Creamy, chewy, and rich—caramels are one of my favorite foods. Choose a coarse sea salt without additives, so you don't have off flavors in your candy. Or use fleur de sel, the gray salt of Brittany, or smoked salt. A probe thermometer set in the saucepan makes this a breeze.

1	cup crème fraîche, homemade (page 12) or store-bought, or heavy (whipping) cream
¾	teaspoon coarse sea salt
½	teaspoon pure vanilla extract
2	cups sugar
⅓	cup light corn syrup
¼	cup water
6	tablespoons (¾ stick) unsalted butter, cut into small pieces

STEP 1 Line an 8-inch square baking pan with 2 sheets of wax paper, leaving an overhang on all sides. Use tape to secure the paper. Generously butter the paper.

STEP 2 Heat the crème fraîche, salt, and vanilla in a small saucepan over medium heat until hot. Set aside, covered to keep warm.

STEP 3 Heat the sugar, corn syrup, and water in a large heavy saucepan over medium heat, stirring, until the sugar is dissolved. Increase the heat to high and bring the mixture to a boil, washing down the sides of the pan with a wet pastry brush if you see any sugar crystals. Boil, without stirring, until the mixture registers 350°F on a probe or candy thermometer.

STEP 4 Remove the pan from the heat and swirl in the butter. Carefully and slowly pour in the crème fraîche mixture. Return the pan to medium-high heat and cook until the thermometer registers 250°F.

STEP 5 Immediately pour the caramel into the prepared pan, without scraping up the caramel from the bottom, which could cause crystallization. Let cool to room temperature on a wire rack.

STEP 6 Using the wax paper, remove the caramel from the pan and invert onto another piece of wax paper. (If it sticks to the pan, place the pan over low heat for a few seconds to loosen it.) Peel off the wax paper. With a buttered very sharp chef's knife, cut the caramel into 64 squares (8 strips in one direction and then 8 in the other). Wrap each caramel in a 4-inch square of cellophane or wax paper, twisting the ends in opposite directions. Store in an airtight container for up to 2 weeks.

praline **truffles**

MAKES ABOUT 24 TRUFFLES

I love these. The crunchy praline inside and coating the outside is the perfect foil for the creamy chocolate, and the praline adds a lovely bittersweet edge. Use praline made with the nut or nuts of your choice.

8   ounces bittersweet or semisweet chocolate, finely chopped

½   cup crème fraîche, homemade (page 12), or store-bought, or heavy (whipping) cream

½   teaspoon pure vanilla extract

     Pinch of salt

½   cup plus 2 tablespoons finely ground Praline (page 144)

STEP 1 Melt the chocolate with the crème fraîche, vanilla, and salt in a heatproof bowl set over a saucepan of about 1 ½ inches of nearly simmering water, whisking until smooth. Remove the bowl from the heat, add the 2 tablespoons praline, and whisk until well combined. Let cool to room temperature, then refrigerate, tightly covered, for at least 2 hours, until thoroughly chilled and set, or for up to 3 days.

STEP 2 Place the remaining ½ cup praline on a small plate. Working quickly, roll a rounded measuring teaspoon of the chocolate mixture into a 1-inch ball in your hands, lightly coat with the praline, and set on another plate. Repeat with the remaining truffle mixture and praline. Store between layers of wax paper in an airtight container in the refrigerator for up to 1 week. Serve at room temperature.

index

table of equivalents

The exact equivalents in the following tables have been rounded for convenience.

LIQUID/DRY MEASUREMENTS

U.S.	METRIC
¼ teaspoon	1.25 milliliters
½ teaspoon	2.5 milliliters
1 teaspoon	5 milliliters
1 tablespoon (3 teaspoons)	15 milliliters
1 fluid ounce (2 tablespoons)	30 milliliters
¼ cup	60 milliliters
⅓ cup	80 milliliters
½ cup	120 milliliters
1 cup	240 milliliters
1 pint (2 cups)	480 milliliters
1 quart (4 cups, 32 ounces)	960 milliliters
1 gallon (4 quarts)	3.84 liters
1 ounce (by weight)	28 grams
1 pound	448 grams
2.2 pounds	1 kilogram

LENGTHS

U.S.	METRIC
⅛ inch	3 millimeters
¼ inch	6 millimeters
½ inch	12 millimeters
1 inch	2.5 centimeters

OVEN TEMPERATURE

FAHRENHEIT	CELSIUS	GAS
250	120	½
275	140	1
300	150	2
325	160	3
350	180	4
375	190	5
400	200	6
425	220	7
450	230	8
475	240	9
500	260	10